Cinnamon
MORNINGS
& Savory
NIGHTS

Other books by Pamela Lanier (published by Lanier Publishing):
The Complete Guide to Bed & Breakfasts, Inns
*   and Guesthouses International*
All-Suite Hotel Guide
Elegant Small Hotels
Condo Vacations: The Complete Guide
Family Travel & Resorts
Golf Resorts: The Complete Guide
22 Days in Alaska

Cinnamon MORNINGS

& Savory NIGHTS

by
Pamela Lanier

LANIER PUBLISHING INTERNATIONAL, LTD.
PETALUMA, CALIFORNTIA

Cover design by Toby Schmidt
Illustrations by Lisa Umlauf-Roese
Interior design by Jacqueline Spadero
Typeset by John Richards

Printed in China on recycled paper

The information in this book was supplied in large part by the inns themselves and is subject to change without notice. We strongly recommend that you call ahead to verify the information presented here before making final plans or reservations. The author and publisher make no representation that this book is accurate or complete. Errors and omissions, whether typographical, clerical, or otherwise, may sometimes occur herein.

This book may not be reproduced in whole or in part in any form or by any means, electronic or mechanical, including photocopying, recording, or by any information storage and retrieval system now known or hereafter invented, without written permission from the publisher.

© 2009 by Lanier Publishing International, Ltd. All rights reserved.
-Published 2009.

ISBN 0-9840850-0-9

This book can be ordered by mail from the publisher. Please include $2.75 for postage and handling for each copy. But try your bookstore first!
Lanier Publishing International, Ltd.
P.O. Box D
Petaluma, CA 94953
Tel.   (707) 763-0271
Fax   (707) 763-5762
email: lanier@travelguides.com

Find us on the internet at
http://www.LanierBB.com
http://www.travelguides.com

The images in this guide are representative of the bed and breakfast lifestyle and cuisine, and do not exactly reflect the recipes in this cookbook.

Acknowledgements

This cookbook is dedicated to the newest members of my family Bob and Savannah Violet.

Many thanks to the cooks who took time to send us their recipes and suggestions and to those inns who provided us with the line drawings of their establishments. Special thanks to all my friends who helped with this book, and especially project coordinators, Ara Armstrong and Megan Reed, culinary editor, Claire Hoepke, and assistant editors, Laurence Blanchette, Justina Long-Am, Marie Castro, technical team, Shannon Holl and Steve Kelez—all of whose excellent work is evident throughout.

Contents

Entrées 96

Bed and breakfast inns (B&B) allow the traveler to be immersed in the elegance of an Antebellum plantation, to sleep in an historic landmark, to get away from it all on a Colorado ranch or to try houseboating in San Francisco. Whatever the setting, the personal and convivial atmosphere of a B&B provides the chance to make new friends and relax while vacationing. All the little B&B extras that one doesn't expect from an impersonal hotel add up to a special travel experience that is winning over all who travel the B&B route.

Of course, food is an essential ingredient in the B&B experience. This cookbook is a collection of innkeepers' favorite recipes of outstanding regional American cuisine, from Southern biscuits and pecan pie to Northeastern blueberry cobbler to Southwestern huevos rancheros. Breakfast, brunch, cocktail hour and desserts are common culinary customs in America's inns; we include B&B dishes to be served throughout the day.

Chocolate desserts, especially, bring out the very best in B&B chefs. This cookbook will tempt the palate with incredible delights such as fudge, brownies, cheesecake, and tortes all blessed with chocolate as their main ingredient. Some will spark the imagination of even the most discriminating gourmet, while others will be perfect for that hectic Sunday when you want to do something special but haven't got much time or energy.

Most of the recipes are simple and easy to prepare, but they cover a wide range of cooking styles from a diverse variety of kitchens. Some chefs are precise and detailed in their instructions; others leave much up to the individual cook. To make the preparations of the dishes easier, we have endeavored to standardize the measurements and procedures—without distracting from the unique style of each contributing chef. In addition to the recipes, we have included a short profile of each inn to help you with your future travel plans. When you visit each inn, you can taste its specialties for yourself.

Bon appetit and sweet dreams!

Introduction

Breakfast

At the heart of every traveler's dreams is an inn where everything possible is done to please the guests. Thanks to abundant fresh produce and the creativity of their kitchens, America's innkeepers have created some of the most imaginative and delicious dishes ever to grace a breakfast table. These recipes offer a glimpse of the diversity of America's regional cuisine. The style, of course, varies from inn to inn, and with the recipes on the following pages, you can create these treats over and over again.

The variety is not just in the food, however. There are just as many kinds of breakfasts as there are inns. Luxury establishments pride themselves on exquisite cuisine graciously presented. Country and small town inns often offer very substantial breakfasts with several choices of entrees, freshly baked fruit breads, juices and cereal.

Other inns provide breakfast at small tables for individual parties, where the food is either served to your exact specifications or is the day's special dish. Of course, food is not the only factor that contributes to an enjoyable eating experience. The mood of the meal is also created by the place setting, the china, the tablecloth, the vase of flowers on the table and the smile on the host or hostess's face.

LA CORSETTE MAISON INN

629 First Ave E
Newton, IA 50208

641-792-6833

EMAIL
lacorsettemaison@aol.com

URL
www.lacorsette.com

LA CORSETTE MAISON INN
Sausage & Wild Rice Casserole

½ cup wild rice
½ cup long grain white rice
2¼ cups water
1 lb bulk sausage meat
One 10½ oz can mushroom
   soup

1 medium onion, finely chopped
1 cup finely chopped celery
1 teaspoon salt
¼ teaspoon pepper

Preheat oven to 350°F.

Cook rices in water for 20 minutes and drain off any excess water. Cook sausage in a pan until crumbly. Pour off extra fat left in the pan. Stir in soup, celery, onion, salt and pepper. Add to rice. Put mixture in buttered casserole. Cover casserole. Bake in 350°F oven for 45 minutes.

Yield: 4 servings

Cooking Time: 2 hr

THE INN AT 410

Chilaquile Casserole

1 tablespoon canola oil
1 small onion, chopped
4 medium zucchini, quartered
    lengthwise and cut in
    chunks
4 medium tomatoes, seeded and
    chopped
1½ teaspoons ground cumin
1 teaspoon dried basil
12 corn tortillas (for a colorful
    touch use a combination
    of yellow and blue corn
    tortillas)

2 4 ounce cans diced green
    chilies, drained
2 cups (8 ounces) shredded low
    fat Monterey Jack cheese
2 cups buttermilk
4 large eggs
¼ teaspoon ground black pepper
Southwest black bean, corn or
    pepper relish or salsa

THE INN AT 410

410 N Leroux St
Flagstaff, AZ 86001

928-774-0088

EMAIL
info@inn410.com

URL
www.inn410.com

THE NIGHT BEFORE:
Heat the canola oil a in large skillet over medium heat, add chopped onion and sauté until soft and translucent, about 5 minutes. Add the chopped zucchini and sauté until tender, about 5 more minutes. Add chopped tomatoes, sprinkle with cumin and basil, and gently stir to mix. Heat until just warm. Set aside to cool.

Spray a 9 × 13 pan with non-stick cooking spray. Tear 6 tortillas into bite-size pieces and spread evenly in prepared pan. Spread 1 can of chilies and 1 cup shredded cheese over tortillas. Next, spread cooled onion-zucchini-tomato mixture evenly over the cheese. Tear remaining tortillas into bite-size pieces and spread over the vegetables. Follow with remaining chilies and cheese. Cover with foil and refrigerate until morning.

IN THE MORNING:
Preheat oven to 375. Remove casserole from refrigerator and uncover. In a medium bowl, whisk together buttermilk, eggs and ground black pepper. Slowly pour over the casserole. Bake uncovered for 35 minutes or until eggs are set. Serve hot, warm or at room temperature with relish or salsa.

Yield: **12 servings**

BLUE LAKE RANCH

16000 Hwy 140
Hesperus, CO 81326

970-385-4537

EMAIL
bluelake@frontier.net

URL
www.bluelakeranch.
com

BLUE LAKE RANCH

Blue Lake Ranch Southwest Scramble

10 whole eggs
1 can cream of mushroom soup
1 cup diced green chili (mild to
    hot)
2 cups grated sharp cheddar
    cheese

6 to 8 large potatoes (red,
    yellow, or white)
Fresh chopped cilantro and
    diced red bell pepper to
    garnish

Preheat oven to 350 degrees. Peel and dice potatoes into bite-sized pieces; mix with mushroom soup and green chili. Season to taste with salt and pepper.

Microwave the mixture for 7–8 minutes in a microwave safe dish. While the potato mixture is cooking in the microwave, scramble the eggs and season to taste with salt and pepper.

Pour the eggs over the potato mix. Sprinkle with the cheddar cheese. Bake in a 350 degree oven until the eggs are set and the cheese is bubbly. Garnish with cilantro and red pepper. Wonderful with fresh salsa and sour cream.

Enjoy!

Wood Violets

GREEN MOUNTAIN INN
Spinach – Mushroom Strudel

GREEN MOUNTAIN
INN

PO Box 60
Stowe, VT 05672

802-253-7301

EMAIL
info@gminn.com

URL
www.
greenmountaininn.com

1 Puff pastry sheet – let sit at room temperature while preparing filling
1 (10 ounce) package of fresh spinach
4 cups of sliced mushrooms

1 (8 ounce) package of cream cheese, cut into cubes
3 tablespoons of butter
Salt to taste
1 egg plus 1 tablespoon water

Preheat oven to 350°F

Cook spinach and mushrooms over medium heat until soft. Take off heat and mix with cream cheese. Place filling in the middle of the puff pastry and fold both sides over the filling. Place on a sheet pan, with the folded side down. Brush with egg wash, (1 egg mixed with 1 tablespoon of water). Bake at 350°F for 20–25 minutes.

Yield: 4

Cooking Time: 30 min.

MAPLE HILL FARM
B&B INN

11 Inn Rd
Hallowell, ME 04347

207-622-2708

EMAIL
stay@MapleBB.com
URL
www.MapleBB.com

M A P L E   H I L L   F A R M   B & B   I N N

Eggs Benedict Arnold

Hollandaise Sauce For About 4 Servings:
3 egg yolks, beaten
1 tablespoon water
1 tablespoon lemon juice
Dash of white pepper & salt
½ cup butter, cut into thirds

Per Serving:
2 farm-fresh free range eggs, poached
2 slices lightly grilled Canadian bacon
1 toasted fork-split English muffin

Prepare Hollandaise sauce in the top of a double boiler, combining egg yolks, water, lemon juice, pepper and salt. Add one piece of the butter and place over boiling water.

Cook, stirring until butter melts and sauce begins to thicken. Add the rest of the butter and continue stirring until it thickens.

Meanwhile, poach two eggs in simmering water until fully cooked on the outside, but with yolks soft. Grill two slices of lean Canadian bacon and place on toasted English muffin halves.

Place drained eggs on top of bacon and slather with Hollandaise sauce. Top with chopped parsley and serve with farm-fried potatoes (use olive oil) and sliced orange garnish. Beautiful and divine!

Yield: 4 servings

Cooking Time: 30 min.

CHRISTOPHER'S B&B

Best Egg Casserole Ever!

CHRISTOPHER'S B&B

604 Poplar St
Bellevue, KY 41073

859-491-9354

EMAIL
christophers@insightbb.
com

URL
www.christophersbb.
com/

12 eggs
1 teaspoon Lawry's seasoned salt (or, to taste)
¾ stick butter or margarine
1 cup plain yogurt
2 cups shredded hash brown potatoes (thawed)
¼ cup (or less) chopped onion
1 cup grated sharp cheddar cheese

Preheat oven to 350°.

Spray or grease a two-quart casserole dish with cooking oil.

Beat eggs, yogurt, and salt together.

Melt butter and lightly sauté onion. Add thawed potatoes. Stir to mix.

Pour in egg mixture and lightly stir to blend ingredients.

Pour into casserole dish. Sprinkle grated cheese over casserole.

Bake at 350° for approximately 30–40 minutes or until knife comes out clean when inserted.

If preparing the dish the night before, bake for approximately 45–50 minutes.

Cut into 8 squares.

Yield: 8 servings

Cooking Time: 30 min.

AMID SUMMER'S INN
B&B

140 South 100 West
Cedar City, UT 84720

435-586-2600

EMAIL
info@amidsummersinn.
com

URL
www.
amidsummersinn.com

AMID SUMMER'S INN B&B

Three Cheese Crustless Quiche

¼ cup butter
½ cup flour
1 cup cream or milk
1 teaspoon baking powder
1 teaspoon salt
1 teaspoon sugar
¼ teaspoon mustard

¼ teaspoon nutmeg
6 large eggs
1 (3 oz.) package softened cream
  cheese
2 cups cottage cheese
1 lb. cubed Monterey Jack
  cheese

Melt butter, add flour until smooth consistency. Beat cream or milk, baking powder, salt, sugar, dry mustard, nutmeg, eggs and cheeses. Add butter and flour mixture. Stir until well blended. (I use a wet towel over my mixer so mixture doesn't fly out everywhere.) Pour into a 9 × 13-inch baking dish that has been sprayed with a no stick cooking spray. Bake at 350 degrees for 45 min to 1 hr. Garnish with sliced red pepper.

   Optional: You may add salsa or green Tabasco sauce on top.

Yield: 10 servings

Cooking Time: 1 hr

GASTHAUS SWITZERLAND INN

Bircher Muesli

2 cups yogurt nature (plain)
2 cups rolled oats
1 cup milk
3-4 spoonfuls of sugar
½ lemon (squeezed)
Stir this together, then add:
2 chopped apples
2 bananas
1 orange
Some grapes, strawberries, or any other fruit such as pears,
pineapple, blueberries, raspberry, kiwi...

Combine everything to your taste. Leave overnight. Add, if you like, some nuts, and raisins or whipped cream!

Health-conscious eating is not a new idea, and in the past many health professionals developed recipes and foods for patients interested in enhancing their health through the foods they ate.

This famous dish was created by Dr. Bircher in 1887 in Switzerland at his diet clinic. In 1924 it was named Bircher-Muesli and became a Swiss national tradition. Next time you see muesli in the stores, you'll know where it came from.

Yield: 6 servings

GASTHAUS
SWITZERLAND INN

89 Daly Ave
Ottawa, ON K1N 6E6
Canada

613-237-0335

EMAIL
info@ottawainn.com

URL
www.ottawainn.com

A DRAGONFLY
RANCH

PO Box 675
Honaunau, HI 96726

808-328-9670

EMAIL
info@dragonflyranch.
com

URL
www.dragonflyranch.
com

A D R A G O N F L Y R A N C H

Hearty Dragonfly Hot Cereal

Soak overnight 2 cups Quinoa (pronounced Keen Wa). In the morning, rinse well (scrunching to get off bitter outer layer of saponas). Put in rice cooker. Add 4 cups boiling hot water (or Celestial Seasonings 'Bengal Spice' Tea for added flavor). Press down 'on' button of rice cooker and wait about 20 minutes. In the meantime, lightly roast 1 cup of pecans in a skillet (no oil) until pecans are fragrant. Allow pecans to cool down. Grind pecans and ½ cup fresh (golden if possible) organic flax seeds (preferably done in a vita mix—but a seed grinder or coffee grinder will do). Combine a few spoonfuls of ground pecan/flax seed with each bowl of cooked quinoa cereal when the cereal has slightly cooled so as to not heat the flax, adding a Tablespoon of fresh refrigerated flax seed oil if desired.

For an extra sweet delight, make a topping: 1 cup of fresh or dried soaked figs, 2 tbsp sesame tahini, ½ tsp mellow white miso. Blend in mixer, adding water, yogurt, or Bengal Spice Tea to desired consistency.

This healthy, yummy breakfast treat was created by our dear friend/frequently returning Dragonflyer, Tracy Holzman, who has joined the staff to organize and cook for retreats and workshops.

FINTON'S LANDING ON KEUKA LAKE

Granola Cereal

1 cup butter or margarine
1 cup packed brown sugar
2 tsp vanilla
6 cups quick oats
6 cups cornflakes or bran flakes
1 cup wheat germ (I use toasted)

1 cup sunflower seeds
1 cup nuts (any kind)
1 cup raisins
dried apricots, dried cranberries, dried dates

FINTON'S LANDING
ON KEUKA LAKE

661 E Lake Rd
Penn Yan, NY 14527

315-536-3146

EMAIL
tepperd@eznet.net

URL
home.eznet.
net/~tepperd

Put first 3 ingredients in medium saucepan. Bring to a boil. Simmer five minutes, stirring occasionally. Place the next 6 ingredients in a large baking pan. Mix well. Pour above hot mixture over dry ingredients. Stir until coated. Cool slightly, then toss the mixture with hands to fully coat. Bake at 350 degrees for about 10 minutes. Remove from oven and stir in the dried fruits. Be creative and add what you like! Allow to completely cool and store in an air-tight container

Yield: 8 servings

HIGHLAWN INN

171 Market St
Berkeley Springs, WV
25411

304-258-5700

EMAIL
info@highlawninn.com

URL
www.highlawninn.com

HIGHLAWN INN
Fruit Oatmeal

2 cups fruit (a mixture of
    sliced peaches, cantalope
    balls, honeydew balls,
    blackberries)
1 cup fruit juice (defrosted
    frozen fruit or orange or
    peach juice)

1 teaspoon ground cinnamon
½ teaspoon ground coriander
½ teaspoon ground allspice
1 tablespoon pure vanilla
1 tablespoon peach schnapps

Topping
1 cup old fashioned oats
½ cup brown sugar

¼ cup butter or margarine
2 tablespoon flour

Preheat oven to 350°F

Place fruit in clear oven-proof dish sprayed with vegetable spray—set aside. In a separate bowl, combine the cinnamon, coriander, allspice, vanilla and schnapps. Stir well until blended. Pour over fruit.

For the topping, cut sugar, butter and flour into oats with a fork in a separate bowl. Press this mixture firmly into center of fruit with back of spoon. (leave about 1 inch around sides uncovered) Bake uncovered at 350 degrees for 30–40 minutes or until center is set and fruit along sides bubbles over.

Yield: 8 servings

Cooking Time: 30 min.

SUNFLOWER HILL LUXURY INN

Sunflower Hill Granola

6 cups regular rolled oats
⅔ cup sunflower seeds
⅓ cup sesame seeds
1⅔ cups (3 oz.) 'ribbon'
    coconut (also referred to as
    'chips')
1½ cups (5 oz.) coarse chopped
    (or sliced) almonds

½ cup butter (1 square)
½ cup brown sugar
½ cup honey
½ t salt
1 t pure vanilla extract

SUNFLOWER HILL
LUXURY INN

185 N 300 E
Moab, UT 84532

435-259-2974

EMAIL
innkeeper@
sunflowerhill.com

URL
www.sunflowerhill.com

Preheat oven to 300 degrees F. In a large stainless steel bowl, mix: oats, sunflower seeds and sesame seeds. In another bowl mix coconut and almonds. In a microwave-safe bowl mix butter, brown sugar, honey and salt. Bake the rolled oat and seed mixture in oven for 6 minutes, stir and bake an additional 6 minutes.

Heat butter and sugar mixture in microwave until butter completely melts, mix thoroughly with a wire whip and then add 1 teaspoon pure vanilla extract (whip together to make a thick sauce).

Add coconut and almonds to the baked oat mixture. Pour contents of microwave bowl over mixture, and stir until entire mixture is coated.

Bake in a 300 degree F oven for 12–15 minutes. Stir mixture every four minutes so granola will toast evenly.

TWO SUNS INN

1705 Bay St
Beaufort, SC 29902

843-522-1122

EMAIL
twosuns@islc.net

URL
www.twosunsinn.com

TWO SUNS INN
Two Suns Crepes with Fruit Glaze

½ cup well sifted flour
½ cup oil
¼ cup milk
4 eggs (or equivalent egg
    substitutes)

Fruit Glaze/Filling:
3+ cups fresh fruit (whole
    strawberries, or cutup

peaches or nectarines work
    well)
1 cup water
⅓ cup sugar
2 tbl cornstarch
lemon juice to taste
food coloring

Crepes

Combine all ingredients and mix at low speed until well blended, then high speed until 'creamy. Preheat a 9 inch omelet pan to hot, remove momentarily from heat, ladle ½ soup ladle, swirl around pan completely, return to heat, count to 10 and flip over gently. Remove pan from heat and swirl pan around gently for a few seconds and remove.

Crepes can be stacked, after cooling to room temperature, with wax paper liner between every four, wrapped tightly in plastic bags, and frozen for later use. This recipe produces a soft crepe which can easily be folded around a fruit glaze filling. Note: Crepe pans are not recommended for this recipe (or any other).

Fruit Glaze/Filling: Thoroughly combine all ingredients, except lemon juice, and stir constantly until cornstarch is fully dissolved in sweetened liquid. Add food coloring (2–3 drops red for strawberries, 2–3 drops red and yellow for peaches, nectarines) to match type of fruit used and bring to full boil until liquid is translucent. Add fresh fruit and cook over low heat for about 5 minutes. Depending on sweetness of fruit used, add 1–3 tbls of lemon juice to produce a slightly sweet/tart taste. Glaze can be thickened or thinned by amount of water used or added.

Yield: Filling for 16–20 crepes with crepes folded in thirds around filling. Dust the filled crepes with powdered sugar and add a spring of parsley or other garnish on top. Complete the plate with a twisted orange slice and several, arranged plum or banana slices.

Yield: 8 servings

G R E E N F I E L D   I N N
Vic's Decadent French Toast

GREENFIELD INN

PO Box 400
Greenfield, NH 03047

603-547-6327

EMAIL
innkeeper@
greenfieldinn.com

URL
www.greenfieldinn.com

2 tbsp corn syrup
1 cup firmly packed brown sugar
5 tbsp margarine or butter
16 slices inexpensive wheat sandwich bread, crusts removed
5 eggs
1½ cups milk
1 tsp vanilla extract
about ½ cup sour cream
1½ cups strawberries, hulled, or 1 oz. pkg. frozen unsweetened
  strawberries, partially thawed

Combine corn syrup, brown sugar and margarine in a small heavy saucepan and heat, stirring, until bubbly. Pour syrup mixture into a 9 × 13 inch pan. Nestle the bread slices into the syrup, making two layers. Mix together eggs, milk and vanilla and pour over the bread. Cover pan and refrigerate overnight. The next morning, remove the pan from the refrigerator and discard the cover. Place pan in a preheated 350 degree oven an bake 45 minutes. To serve, loosen edges of bread from pan sides with the blade of a knife or a thin blade spatula. Invert the pan onto a serving plate so that the caramelized portion of the french toast is on top. Divide into serving portions and top each serving with a tbsp of sour cream and some strawberries. Serve immediately.

Yield: 8 servings

BREWERY GULCH INN

9401 North Highway
One
Mendocino, CA 95460

707-937-4752

EMAIL
innkeeper@
brewerygulchinn.com

URL
www.brewerygulchinn.
com

B R E W E R Y   G U L C H   I N N
Brioche French Toast

1 cup half & half
2 eggs
1 tablespoon sugar
Pinch cinnamon
Pinch mace
Pinch cardamon
Pinch salt
12 slices day old brioche (thick sliced)

For the fruit sauté:
2 tablespoons butter
2 tablespoons Granny Smith apples (diced)
1 tablespoon cranberries
1 tablespoon toasted walnuts
1 tablespoon light brown sugar
2 teaspoons Grand Marnier
For the vanilla-Bourbon Maple Syrup:
3 vanilla beans (split in half)
2 tablespoon of dark bourbon
1 cup high quality maple syrup

Combine half and half, eggs, sugar, cinnamon, mace, cardamom, and salt and mix them into a smooth batter. Heat a nonstick skillet over medium heat with a teaspoon of butter.

Dip the bread into the batter coating both sides evenly. Fry the slices on one side until evenly browned and then turn and brown the other side. Serve immediately. Top with sautéed apples, cranberries, and walnuts or warm vanilla-bourbon maple syrup.

Fruit Sauté:
Lightly sauté the apples in 1 tablespoon of butter over medium heat until starting to brown. Next add cranberries, walnuts, and sugar. Gently sauté until all the sugar has caramelized. Deglaze the pan with Grand Marnier and incorporate last tablespoon of butter, being careful not to let it separate. Pour over Brioche French Toast and enjoy!

Vanilla-Bourbon Maple Syrup:
Split the vanilla beans scraping out the seeds and flambe the beans and seeds in bourbon. Combine with high quality maple syrup and pour over Brioche French Toast.

Yield: 6

CANDLELIGHT INN B&B

Creme Caramel French Toast

CANDLELIGHT INN
B&B

2574 Lincoln Hwy E
Ronks, PA 17572

717-299-6005

EMAIL
candleinn@aol.com

URL
www.candleinn.com

2 tbsp light corn syrup
¼ cup butter
1½ lbs. cinnamon raisin bread
2 cups light cream
2 tsp vanilla
sour cream

1 cup brown sugar
6 eggs
2 cups milk
⅓ cup sugar
½ tsp salt

In a saucepan combine the corn syrup, brown sugar, and butter. Melt until smooth and bubbly. Spread in the bottom of an 11 × 17 in. glass baking pan. Overlap bread slices like dominos in pan over syrup. In a bowl mix eggs, milk, light cream, sugar, vanilla, and salt. Bake at 350 degrees for 45 minutes, then remove foil. Bake for 10–15 more minutes or until puffed and golden brown. Slice and invert pieces to serve. Garnish with sour cream.

CANDLELIGHT INN

2310 Central Ave
North Wildwood, NJ
08260

609-522-6200

EMAIL
info@candlelight-inn.
com

URL
www.candlelight-inn.
com

CANDLELIGHT INN
Raisin Bread French Toast

10 eggs
2 cups half-and-half
½ cup heavy cream
¾ cup B&B Benedictine
3 teaspoons vanilla extract
⅓ cup sugar
¼ teaspoon fresh ground
   nutmeg
¼ teaspoon fresh ground
   cinnamon
1 teaspoon grated orange peel
¼ pound unsalted butter
16 slices (½ inch) Raisin Bread
3 cups strawberry coulis

Beat eggs, then mix in half-and-half, cream, B&B, sugar, nutmeg, vanilla, cinnamon, and orange peel. Dip raisin bread slices in batter, one at a time, until soaked. Apply ¼ of butter to skillet over medium heat. Fry 4–6 slices, depending on size of skillet, at a time until golden brown on each side. Remove to platter and keep warm. Add more butter to skillet and repeat process until all bread slices are fried. Place 2 slices on serving dish, one half overlapping the other.

Warm coulis in separate sauce pan. Pour ⅓ cup strawberry coulis along side of toast. Garnish coulis with sliced almonds and sprinkle powdered sugar on toast.

Strawberry Coulis (makes approximately one quart):
4 pounds fresh of frozen strawberries
1½ cups sugar
½ cup B&B Benedictine

Puree strawberries in blender. Pour into sauce pan, stir in sugar. Bring to slow boil over medium heat. When coulis begins to boil, turn heat down to allow coulis to simmer. Skim off froth on top of mixture. Continue to simmer for five minutes. Add B&B and simmer for five more minutes. Cool and store in refrigerator.

Yield: 8 servings

CAPTAIN SCHOONMAKER'S
B & B

To Die For French Toast

½ cup melted butter
½ cup brown sugar
1 Tbsp. cinnamon
2 Granny Smith Apples (Peeled
& Sliced)
1 Loaf Homebaked Bread
(crusts removed & thickly
sliced)

6 eggs
1 tsp. vanilla
Grated nutmeg
1½ cups milk or half & half

CAPTAIN
SCHOONMAKER'S
B&B

913 State Rte 213
High Falls, NY 12440

845-687-7946

EMAIL
schoonmkr1@aol.com

URL
www.
captainschoonmakers.
com

Mix melted butter, brown sugar and cinnamon, in bottom of 9 × 9 inch baking pan. Cover with layer of sliced apples. Layer thick bread slices on top, making 2 layers. Mix eggs with vanilla and nutmeg and milk and pour over layers. Cover and refrigerate overnight. Bake at 350 for about 45 minutes until golden. Serve inverted so apples are on top, sprinkle with powdered sugar.

EAGLES NEST INN

4680 Saratoga Rd
Langley, WA 98260

360-221-5331

EMAIL
eaglnest@whidbey.com

URL
www.eaglesnestinn.
com

E A G L E S   N E S T   I N N

Crispy Pecan Praline French Toast

3 eggs
1½ cup milk
1½ cup Krustease baking mix (or Bisquick)
1 tsp. vanilla
1 tsp. cinnamon
2 loaves French or sourdough bread

Praline mix:
1½ cups crushed corn flakes
1 cup brown sugar
1 cup finely chopped pecans

Blend first 5 ingredients and refrigerate over night.

Cut your favorite loaf on bread in slices about 1 inch thick 1 hr. before serving. Dip the bread slices into the batter to coat each side, then stand them back to form the loaf shape again. (Do not soak in the batter). Let stand approx. 30 minutes.

Make praline mix and place in a wide pie plate.

Dip each side of battered bread in praline mixture. Brown French toast in skillet or on hot griddle with melted margarine until golden brown. Serve with favorite syrup. I use maple and flavor it with orange zest. Note: Left over praline mix can be stored air tight for later use.

Yield: 8 servings

ROSE COTTAGE GUEST HOUSE
Lemon Cream Cheese French Toast

ROSE COTTAGE GUEST HOUSE

1929 Austin Rd NE
Tacoma, WA 98422

253-927-9437

EMAIL
info@
rosecottageguesthouse.
com

URL
www.
rosecottageguesthouse.
com

Cream Cheese Filling:
*8 ounces of low or no fat soft
    cream cheese*
1½ tablespoons lemon juice
Zest of one lemon
⅓ cup sugar
*1 loaf of packaged, plain, sliced
    French Bread (small sized
    loaf)*

Egg Batter:
6 eggs or egg beater equivalent
2½ cups of non-fat half & half
⅓ cup sugar
2 teaspoons vanilla extract
*1 teaspoon fresh ground
    nutmeg*

Warm Orange Sauce:
½ cup fresh orange juice
1 tablespoon sugar
*1 cup fresh quartered
    strawberries*

Stir together in a small bowl the cream cheese, lemon juice, zest and sugar. Set aside. Blend the egg, half & half, sugar, vanilla and nutmeg in a large flat bottom bowl. Set aside. Using two slices of the French bread, spread about 2 tablespoons of the cream cheese filling on one side. Place other slice on top and lightly press together. Dip the sandwich into the batter, turn once and place on a lightly oiled griddle that has been preheated on medium heat. Cook until lightly browned on each side, about 3 minutes. Serve warm with your favorite topping or the warm orange/strawberry sauce.

Warm Orange Sauce:
Heat in a small pan over low heat, orange juice and sugar till dissolved. Add strawberries and just barely warm. Place in a serving bowl to spoon over the French Toast.

Serve with thin sliced low fat slices of ham. Hot maple syrup or powdered sugar sprinkled on top can also be used.

Yield: 6 servings

RIVER RUN B&B INN

PO Box 9
Fleischmanns, NY
12430

845-254-4884

EMAIL
info@riverrun
bedandbreakfast.com

URL
www.riverrun
bedandbreakfast.com

R I V E R   R U N   B & B   I N N

River Run Baked French Toast

1 cup brown sugar
1 stick butter, ½ cup
2 tablespoons maple syrup
1 loaf crusty French bread
8 eggs

2 cups milk
1 tablespoon cinnamon
1 tablespoon vanilla extract
½ cup your favorite liquor

Melt the brown sugar, butter and syrup in a saucepan until bubbly. Pour into a greased 9 × 13 pan. Slice the bread in about 1 inch slices. Beat the remaining ingredients. Dip the slices of bread in the egg mixture and arrange in the pan. Pour remaining egg mixture over the bread. Soak overnight.

Bake in morning at 350°F for 45 minutes. Dust with powdered sugar.

Yield: 8 servings

Cooking Time: 45 min.

BERRY PATCH

Strawberry Stuffed French Toast

4 Thick slices of bakery style
   bread
Strawberry Jam
Cream Cheese – Softened

6 eggs
½ Tbsp. vanilla

On two slices of bread spread a thick layer of cream cheese. On the other two slices of bread spread a thick layer of jam. Make a cream cheese and jam sandwich. Beat 6 eggs and vanilla. Dip each sandwich in the batter. Place on medium setting on greased frying pan and cook until browned evenly on both sides. Cut into triangle pieces and heavily sprinkle with powdered sugar, Top with freshly sliced strawberries.

Yield: 2 servings

BERRY PATCH

115 Moore Rd
Hershey, PA 17046

717-865-7219

EMAIL
bunny@berrypatchbnb.
com

URL
www.berrypatchbnb.
com

MULBERRY B&B

257 High St
Wareham, MA 02571

508-295-0684

EMAIL
mulberry257@comcast.
net

URL
www.virtualcities.com/
ons/ma/z/maza801.
htm

MULBERRY B & B

Mulberry's 10th Anniversary French Toast

For each serving:
2 slices white bread   *2 tablespoons milk*
Cream cheese   *Butter*
Strawberry or raspberry jam   *Bluberry sauce*
1 egg

2 slices of quality white bread. Spread soft cream cheese on each slice. Spread strawberry or raspberry jam on one slice and make a sandwich. Dip in French Toast batter of one egg and 2 tablespoons milk. Brown in melted butter. Serve with blueberry sauce.

Yield: 1 serving

ANGEL'S WATCH INN

Angel Eyes

1 slice per guest of Black Forest
    or Virginia Ham
1 egg per guest
about ¼ cup per guest of
    any vegetable: zucchini,
    summer squash,
    mushrooms, onions, red/
    green pepper, or your
    choice

fresh or dried tarragon
1 tablespoon per guest sour
    cream
½ stick butter
Pepper to taste

ANGEL'S WATCH INN

902 Boston Post Rd
Westbrook, CT 06498

860-399-8846

EMAIL
info@angelswatchinn.
com

URL
www.angelswatchinn.
com

Preheat oven to 450°F

Spray a regular size muffin tin well with cooking spray. Cut up all of your different vegetables into small pieces; sauté them in the butter with tarragon and pepper to taste until they are tender.

When vegetables are tender, stir in sour cream. Take one slice of ham and fit it into each muffin tin, making a nest. Put about one tablespoon of the vegetable mixture into each ham nest. Crack each egg and place on top of the vegetables.

Garnish with tarragon and bake for about 15 minutes until yolks are hard. If you like the yolk runny, bake less. (When feeding the public it is required to cook the yolk longer). Remove from tin and serve on separate dishes with english muffins or fresh biscuits.

Yield: 1 servings

EAGLES NEST INN

4680 Saratoga Rd
Langley, WA 98260

360-221-5331

EMAIL
eaglnest@whidbey.com

URL
www.eaglesnestinn.
com

EAGLES NEST INN
Broccoli & Cheese Souffle

10 eggs, separated
6 tablespoons butter
6 tablespoons flour
1 cup milk
1 teaspoon salt
½ cup chopped green onion
½ cup shredded, then chopped carrot

16 oz. frozen chopped broccoli, thawed
1½ cup cheddar cheese
½ cup parmesan cheese
½ teaspoon mustard
¼ teaspoon tarragon

Preheat oven to 350 degrees.

Separate the eggs. Place egg white in very large bowl. Set aside until later. In a 2 qt. saucepan melt the butter. Then add the onion, carrot, spices and herbs. Cook until tender. Add the flour and cook until absorbed. Add milk and cook until thickened. Puree the broccoli through the food processor and add to the sauce. Next add the cheeses. Remove from the heat and add the egg yolks one at a time. Set aside.

Beat the egg whites stiff but not dry. Just until they form peaks with a slight drop at the top. Stir about ⅓ of the egg white mixture into the sauce. Then transfer the rest of the sauce into the egg whites and fold to blend.

Spray individual 4-inch soufflé dishes with a non-stick coating and fill to within 1/8 inch of the top. Bake in the oven for 25–30 minutes until golden brown on top.

Yield: 10 servings

Cooking Time: 30 min.

BENT   CREEK   LODGE

Smoked Cheese, Leek & Red Pepper Strata

2 tablespoons butter
2 medium red peppers, small diced
2 leeks, white part only, sliced
1 loaf focaccia bread, cubed in ½ inch cubes
1 cup mild smoked cheese, grated—we use smoked Amish yogurt
    cheese
1½ cups milk
1½ cups half & half (half milk, half cream)
9 large eggs, slightly beaten
2 tablespoons Dijon mustard
½ teaspoon salt
½ teaspoon freshly ground black pepper

Sauté peppers and leeks in butter until soft. Set aside. Spread half the bread cubes in a 9 × 13 inch pan that has been sprayed with pan spray.

Top with ¾ of the cheese and ¾ of the leek and pepper mixture. Repeat layers: bread cubes, cheese, pepper/leek mixture.

In a medium bowl, whisk together the milk, half & half, eggs, Dijon, salt & pepper. Pour over bread. Cover and chill in refrigerator overnight if desired. Bake uncovered at 350°F for 45–60 minutes.

Yields: One 9 × 13 inch baking pan

Yield: 8

BENT CREEK LODGE

10 Parkway Crescent
Asheville, NC 28704

828-654-9040

EMAIL
bentcreek@ioa.com

URL
www.bentcreeknc.com

HOLDEN HOUSE 1902
BED & BREAKFAST
INN

1102 W Pikes Peak Ave
Colorado Springs, CO
80904

719-471-3980

EMAIL
mail@holdenhouse.com

URL
www.holdenhouse.com

HOLDEN HOUSE 1902 BED & BREAKFAST INN

Sallie's Special Eggs Goldenrod

24 Peppridge Farm Puff Pastry Shells
2 pkgs white sauce mix (for 2 cups)
12 hard boiled eggs, chopped
Salt and pepper
Tarragon for garnish
Paprika for garnish

Prepare the pastry shells as directed on the package. Pre-boil the eggs the night before if desired. While pastry shells are baking, prepare the white sauce and keep warm on the stove.

Wash the fresh tarragon (dried can be used if necessary), dry and set aside. When the pastry shells are puffed and slightly brown, remove from oven.

Place on plates and remove scored top from shell. Cover chopped eggs with plastic wrap and heat until warm in the microwave (about 1–2 minutes).

Spoon chopped eggs over and into pastry shells. Liberally drizzle white sauce over puff pastry shells. Sprinkle a dash of paprika, salt, pepper, and tarragon over the shells.

Garnish the plate with colorful fruit such as apple and orange slices, small grape bunches, etc., and serve.

Yield: 12 servings

WHISTLING SWAN INN

Curried Eggs in Tomatoes

12 large ripe tomatoes (not
    Beefsteak, though)
1 tsp. Per tomato of White
    Worcestershire sauce
1 tsp. Dill
12 large eggs

1 tsp. Chives (optional)
1 tsp. Thyme (optional)
¼ tsp. Per tomato of curry
¾ cup Parmesan cheese, freshly
    grated (optional)

Spray pan with non-stick cooking spray. Cut off the top of each tomato. If necessary, cut a very thin slice off bottom of each tomato to make a flat base so they won't flip over. Carefully scoop out enough pulp to leave room for each egg.

Option 1: Shake the 1 tsp. of Worcestershire sauce and ¼ tsp. of curry into each tomato cup. Break an egg into each tomato cup. Sprinkle dill on top.

Option 2: Break an egg into tomato cup. Sprinkle each egg with 1 tbsp. Parmesan cheese and each of herbs suggested above.

Bake in a 350 degree oven for 40 minutes, or until eggs have set but are not hard. Serve immediately.

WHISTLING SWAN
INN

110 Main St
Stanhope, NJ 07874

973-347-6369

EMAIL
info@whistlingswaninn.
com

URL
www.
whistlingswaninn.com

CARTER HOUSE INNS

301 L St
Eureka, CA 95501

707-444-8062

EMAIL
reserve@carterhouse.
com

URL
www.carterhouse.com

CARTER HOUSE INNS
Vegetable Omelet in Puff Pastry

For omelet:
Puff pastry dough
5 fresh eggs
1 cup heavy cream
¼ cup onions, chopped
½ cup spinach, chopped
⅓ cup red bell peppers, chopped
⅓ cup zucchini, chopped
⅛ cup ricotta cheese

For Hollandaise Sauce:
3 egg yolks
2 dashes white pepper
1 dash cayenne pepper
½ cube unsalted butter
Juice of ½ lemon
¼ teaspoon salt

Preheat oven to 350°F. Lightly grease a large tart pan.

Take a circular cut-out of pastry dough and lay it on the bottom of the pan so that it conforms to the pan and reaches up the sides.

Whip together eggs and cream. Top the dough with egg/cream mixture. Add onions, spinach, peppers, zucchini, and cheese.

Place another layer of puff pastry over the top of these ingredients and form a pouch around the filling. Bake for 30 minutes.

In a double boiler, whip egg yolks and lemon juice until the mixture has a custard like consistency. Add salt and both peppers.

In a separate pan, melt butter and add it slowly to the mixture, whipping constantly.

When the pastry is removed from the oven, cover it with Hollandaise sauce and serve.

GODDARD MANSION B & B

Cheesie Breakfast Souffle

9 eggs (or egg substitute),
  beaten or whisked
1½ cups milk (whole, 1% or
  2%)
2-3 teaspoons sugar
1–1½ teaspoons salt
12 ounces grated cheese
  (Monterey Jack or
  pregrated, 4-cheese
  Mexican combo)

4½ ounces cream cheese
  (regular or lowfat) cubed or
  cut into small chunks
12 ounces cottage cheese (lowfat
  or nonfat)
1½ teaspoons baking powder
¾ cup flour (white or a blend
  with whole grain flour)
4 tablespoons butter, melted
dash of dill, parsley, paprika
  (optional)

Mix first 7 ingredients together, (may store this portion overnight in refrigerator). Mix baking powder and flour. With whisk, mix dry ingredients into wet mixture, lightly but thoroughly. Last, stir in butter and pour into lightly buttered or oiled 9 × 13 inch baking dish (oval or rectangular).

Optional: Before placing in oven, sprinkle in diagonal lines—dried dill, parsley, and/or paprika in opposite diagonals to make lattice pattern. Bake at 325 degrees for 40–50 minutes, or until lightly browned and knife comes out clean when inserted in the center.

Pretty with green and red for christmas breakfast or brunch.

Yield: 6 servings

GODDARD MANSION
B&B

25 Hillstead Rd
Claremont, NH 03743

603-543-0603

EMAIL
info@goddardmansion.
com

URL
www.goddardmansion.
com

FLERY MANOR B&B

2000 Jumpoff Joe Cr Rd
Grants Pass, OR 97526

541-476-3591

EMAIL
flery@flerymanor.com

URL
www.flerymanor.com

F L E R Y   M A N O R   B & B

Egg on a Cloud

6 eggs, carefully separated
6 toasted rounds, cut from your favorite bread
Your favorite Hollandaise sauce recipe

Preheat oven to 350 degrees F. Toast bread rounds and place on baking sheet. Whip egg whites until stiff peaks form. Divide egg whites over rounds, and with the back of a spoon form a hollow in the center of each. Place yolk (the yellow part) in the hollow. Bake in oven, being careful not to over cook. Cook until yolk is set and white is lightly browned (about 15 minutes). Serve topped with Hollandaise sauce and a dash of paprika.

If you are looking for that special breakfast recipe that will impress your guests, but is easy to prepare, this elegant egg dish is for you! Our version of an old classic. At the Flery Manor, we serve our dish with fresh poached salmon from our local Rogue River; our guests may have caught it themselves.

Yield: 6 servings

THE INN & SPA AT INTERCOURSE VILLAGE

Egg Strudel

THE INN & SPA
AT INTERCOURSE
VILLAGE

PO Box 598
Intercourse, PA 17534

717-768-2626

EMAIL
innkeeper@inn-spa.com

URL
www.
amishcountryinns.
com/inn/index.htm

For egg strudel:
1 sheet frozen puff pastry,
    thawed
6 large eggs
2 tablespoons milk or half and
    half
½ teaspoon salt
¼ teaspoon black pepper
¼ cup chopped tomatoes

¼ cup shredded Swiss cheese

For spinach cream sauce:
1 Tbsp. butter
1 cup frozen spinach, does not
    need to be thawed
2 Tbsp. flour, all purpose
1 to 2 cups milk, whole is best
¼ tsp. grated nutmeg
Salt and pepper to taste

For egg wash:
1 egg

1 Tbsp. milk, half/half, or water

Preheat oven to 375°F.

For the egg strudel, whisk together the 6 eggs, milk, salt and pepper. Place in a heated skillet and scramble till soft scrambled (not well done). Remove from heat.

Make an egg wash by whisking the egg and milk together in a bowl. Unroll the puff pastry sheet and lay out on counter with longest side facing you. Brush the top edge of pastry sheet with the egg wash. Place scrambled eggs ½ inch from the bottom of the puff pastry sheet. Sprinkle the tomatoes and Swiss cheese across the eggs.

Starting at the lower edge, roll pastry away from you, and press the seam. Place seam side down on a parchment lined baking sheet. Brush top w/ egg wash and sprinkle lightly with salt. Bake for 20–30 minutes or until pastry is golden brown.

Cut into desired size, I recommend 6 slices, giving two slices per serving. Top with heated spinach cream sauce.

Spinach Cream Sauce: Melt butter in a nonstick skillet. Add frozen spinach & sauté until spinach is heated through and some of the water has evaporated. Sprinkle in the flour and stir into the spinach cooking for 2 min. Add the milk and nutmeg. Cook over med. heat till sauce thickens. Season to taste with salt & pepper.

Yield: 3 servings   Cooking Time: 30 min.

THE WINE COUNTRY INN & GARDENS

Sourdough Eggs

THE WINE COUNTRY
INN & GARDENS

1152 Lodi Ln
St. Helena, CA 94574

707-963-7077

EMAIL
jim@winecountryinn.
com

URL
www.winecountryinn.
com

12 slices of lightly buttered
*   extra-sourdough bread*
4 cups grated cheddar cheese
½ medium onion diced
1 cup thinly sliced mushrooms
10 eggs

4 cups milk
3 heaping tablespoons of spicy
*   mustard*
1 teaspoon salt
¼ teaspoon pepper

Preheat oven to 325°F

Cut bread into small cubes. Place ½ of bread cubes into large coated baking dish. Sprinkle with 2 cups cheese, onion, and mushrooms. Add second layer of bread and top with remaining cheese.

    Beat eggs, milk, mustard, salt and pepper together. Pour this mixture evenly over the casserole. Cover with foil and refrigerate overnight. Bake at 325° for approximately 50 minutes until top is golden and lightly crusted.

Yield: 6 servings

Cooking Time: 30 min.

GRAY GOOSE INN

Baked Eggs Santa Fe Style

10 eggs
½ cup flour
½ teaspoon salt
2 cups small curd cottage
    cheese
4 cups Monterey Jack cheese
    (grated)
¼ pound butter

4 ounce diced, seeded green
    chilies (hot or mild to taste)
¼ cup chopped red pimiento
8 ounce can whole corn
    (drained)
french fried onions (garnish)
Salsa, mild or hot
    (accompaniment)

Preheat oven to 350°F. Beat eggs until light. Add remaining ingredients except for onions and salsa; mix well. Pour into buttered individual small baking dishes. Bake in preheated oven 35 minutes. About 10 minutes before done, sprinkle onions on top of eggs, continue to bake until done. Serve immediately with salsa on the side.

Yield: 10 servings

GRAY GOOSE INN

350 Indian Boundary
Rd
Chesterton, IN 46304

219-926-5781

EMAIL
graygoose@verizon.net

URL
www.graygooseinn.
com

AMBER HOUSE B&B

1315 22nd St
Sacramento, CA 95816

916-444-8085

EMAIL
info@amberhouse.com

URL
www.amberhouse.com

AMBER HOUSE B & B

Swiss Mustard Eggs

Per serving:
1 English Muffin, toasted
3 eggs
¼ cup grated Swiss cheese
2 Tbls. milk

1 Tbls. stone-ground mustard
1 Tbls. grated parmesan
2 strips bacon
½ tsp pepper

Mix eggs with milk, mustard, and pepper, using wire whisk. Cook bacon till crisp, crumble and set aside. Spread muffin with butter and toast under broiler. Melt ½ tbls butter in skillet. Add egg mixture and scramble. When almost done add Swiss cheese and bacon. Cook till cheese melts. Place muffin on plate, spoon eggs onto both halves, sprinkle with the parmesan. Garnish plate with quartered tomato.

EARLYSTOWN   MANOR
Spinach Omelet Roll

EARLYSTOWN MANOR

Boalsburg, PA 16828
814-466-6481
EMAIL
zxs@psu.edu
URL
www.earlystownmanor.
com

1 cup milk
2 Tbsp. olive oil
7 large eggs
2 tsp. minced garlic
½ cup all-purpose flour
1 lb. fresh or 10 oz. frozen
    spinach
¼ C. unsalted butter
1 cup shredded cheese
    (Gorgonzola, feta, sharp
    cheddar or a combination of
    cheeses)
2 Tbsp. chopped parsley
1 sm. onion chopped

Optional fillings:
*Crumbled bacon (12 oz.
    package), or chopped
    sausage (8 oz.)*

Preheat oven to 400 degrees. Grease a 17 × 12 inch jellyroll pan with solid shortening. Line with parchment paper and grease again. Whisk milk, eggs, flour and butter together in a mixing bowl until well combined and frothy. Stir in parsley. Pour into jellyroll pan and bake for 18–20 minutes, until the roll is just set and slightly puffed. Meanwhile, heat oil in a large skillet. Add garlic and cook for 30 seconds. Add spinach in small batches and cook until slightly wilted. Add additional oil if necessary. If using frozen spinach in place of fresh, cook according to package direction and squeeze out all the water. Remove the roll from the oven and spread spinach evenly over roll. Sprinkle cheese and onions over spinach. Add the bacon or sausage. Roll up omelet without the parchment paper. Bake the omelet roll at 400 degrees for 3–5 minutes until the cheese is melted, or it can be refrigerated overnight and baked the following morning. Remove omelet roll from refrigerator at least 30 minutes before baking. Bake omelet roll at 350 degrees for 15–20 minutes or until the cheese is melted and the filling is hot. Slice into 6–8 pieces to serve.

Yield: 8 servings

CAPTAIN FAIRFIELD
INN

PO Box 3089
Kennebunkport, ME
04046

207-967-4454

EMAIL
rlb@captainfairfield.
com

URL
www.captainfairfield.
com

CAPTAIN FAIRFIELD INN
Skillet Frittata with Seasonal Vegetables

1 red sweet pepper
1 green bell pepper
1 yellow or orange sweet pepper
1 summer squash (medium)
1 zucchini (medium)
1 Spanish onion, coarsely
    chopped
3 ripe Italian plum tomatoes

1 clove fresh garlic, minced
Sprigs of fresh parsley
2 tablespoons olive oil
oregano and thyme
12 eggs
1 cup sharp cheddar cheese
freshly ground black pepper

Cut peppers, summer squash, and zucchini into thin ½ inch strips. Dice the onion and tomatoes into ¼ inch cubes. Peel and finely mince garlic, and finely chop parsley. Heat a medium size pot with olive oil over medium heat, lightly sauté the chopped garlic and onion until translucent. Add freshly cut vegetables, but do not add tomatoes. Add oregano and thyme, and gently toss. Keep vegetables firm, do not overcook.

Remove from heat, add tomatoes, but do not stir. Pour beaten eggs (use 2 beaten eggs for each individual serving) into heated and lightly buttered skillet. Once eggs begin to set, add vegetables to the top.

Arrange colors, do not stir. Add parsley, and then top with cheddar cheese and black pepper (salt optional). Cover and cook over low heat until cheese is melted. Loosen and slide onto warm plate. Serve with French bread cut into triangular thirds and a sprig of fresh parsley.

Yield: 8 servings

MARTINE INN

Castroville Eggs

Sauce:
4 cups cream or half & half
1 teaspoon salt
¼ teaspoon white pepper
¼ cup chopped green onions
¼ cup diced pimentos
2 teaspoons cornstarch
    dissolved in 2 teaspoons
    water
1½ cups shredded cheese of
    your choice (a white cheese
    is recommended)

2½ cups chopped artichoke
    hearts (packed in water, not
    marinated)

Hot water for poaching eggs
    (adding a splash of vinegar
    to the water will keep the
    eggs from spreading)
8 eggs

4 English muffins—split and
    toasted

Mix sauce ingredients in top pan of double boiler. Heat through and add cheese. Heat until cheese melts. Add artichoke hearts. Keep warm in double boiler.

Poach eggs. Place one on each half of English muffin. Ladle sauce over eggs. Garnish with edible flower, parsley or paprika.

Yield: 4 servings

MARTINE INN

PO Box 330
Pacific Grove, CA 93950

831-373-3388

EMAIL
don@martineinn.com

URL
www.martineinn.com

C.W. WORTH HOUSE
B&B

412 S 3rd St
Wilmington, NC 28401

910-762-8562

EMAIL
relax@worthhouse.com

URL
www.worthhouse.com

C . W .   W O R T H   H O U S E   B & B

Spinach & Cheese Croissant Strata

*8 large croissants, torn into
    bite-sized pieces
2 cups shredded cheese
1 box frozen spinach, thawed
    and squeezed dry
8 eggs
2 cups milk*

*hot sauce to taste
Worcestershire sauce
1 teaspoon chopped fresh
    herbs—any you have
    on hand such as basil,
    rosemary, sage, marjoram,
    etc.*

Layer torn croissant pieces in a lightly greased pan, 9 × 13 inch. Layer 1 cup cheese on top of the croissants, and top with spinach. Mix eggs, milk, remaining 1 cup cheese, and seasonings together. Pour over casserole.

Cover loosely with tin foil sprayed with baking spray. Bake in a 350 degree oven for 15 minutes. Then remove the tin foil and rotate the pan for more even baking.

Bake 30 more minutes. Watch that it doesn't brown too much; cover again with tin foil if browning too quickly. It will puff up during the last 10 minutes. A knife inserted in the center should come out clean.

Remove from oven and let rest for 5 minutes before cutting into 8 pieces.

Yield: 8 servings

WILLIAMSBURG SAMPLER B & B INN

Skip Lunch Breakfast

WILLIAMSBURG
SAMPLER B&B INN

922 Jamestown Rd
Williamsburg, VA 23185

757-253-0398

EMAIL
info@
williamsburgsampler.
com

URL
www.
williamsburgsampler.
com

5 tablespoons butter, separated
2 tablespoons flour
2 cups milk
½ teaspoon salt
½ teaspoon pepper
1 4-ounce can mushrooms,
    drained
½ cup shredded American
    cheese
1 cup chopped Canadian bacon
¼ cup chopped green onions
Paprika
1 dozen eggs, beaten
Bread crumbs

Combine 2 tablespoons butter and flour. Blend until smooth. Cook over low heat until bubbly. Gradually stir in milk. Cook until smooth and thick, stirring constantly. Add salt, pepper, and cheese. Heat and stir until cheese melts. Set aside. Sauté bacon and onions in remaining butter until onions are tender. Add eggs; cook until set, stirring to scramble. Fold in mushrooms and cheese sauce. Spoon egg mixture into lightly greased 12-by-7 inch baking dish. Top with bread crumbs; sprinkle with paprika. Bake at 350 degrees for 30 minutes.

Yield: 8 servings

DOMAINE
MADELEINE

146 Wildflower Ln
Port Angeles, WA 98362

360-457-4174

EMAIL
stay@
domainemadeleine.com

URL
www.
domainemadeleine.com

DOMAINE MADELEINE
Apple Souffle Pancake

*3 granny smith apples, peeled,
cored and sliced thick*
7 egg whites, beaten
4 egg yolks
1 cup of flour
1 cup of milk
*¼ cup of Cavados (apple
brandy)*

*¼ teaspoon orange essence, or 1
teaspoon triple sec*
*about ½ cup of golden raisins
soaked in Grand Marnier*
*about ½ cup of chopped
bananas*
about ½ cup toasted pecans

Mix milk, egg yolks and flour together in a large bowl. Season with a dash of salt, a teaspoon or so of vanilla and a teaspoon or so of orange essence and if desired a dash or more of cinnamon.

Set aside this mixture to soak.

Using a high sided skillet, sauté the apples in a small amount of unsalted butter and if you wish a bit of virgin olive oil.

Add some apple brandy if you wish (cook for about one minute to evaporate the alcohol). Add a bit of sugar.

Beat egg whites until stiff, (soft peaks). Fold into the milk-flour-egg yolk mixture, one half at a time.

Pour the batter over the apples in the high-sided skillet you have sautéd the apples in. Add the raisins, bananas, and pecans. (Or the bananas, raisins and pecans may be added first, pouring the batter over them.)

Bake in a 375 degree oven for about 30 minutes or until done. Serve at once.

GRAY GOOSE INN

Heartland Pumpkin Pancakes

2 cups flour
2 Tbsp. brown sugar
1 Tbsp. baking powder
1 tsp. salt and cinnamon
¼ tsp. nutmeg and ginger

½ cup milk
½ cup canned pumpkin
1 egg
2 Tbsp. vegetable oil

In large bowl, combine dry ingredients. In small bowl, combine milk, pumpkin, eggs and oil, stir into flour mixture until dry ingredients are moistened. Batter will be thick. Serve with real Maple syrup.

Yield: 8 servings

GRAY GOOSE INN

350 Indian Boundary Rd
Chesterton, IN 46304

219-926-5781

EMAIL
graygoose@verizon.net

URL
www.graygooseinn.com

GRAY GOOSE INN

350 Indian Boundary
Rd
Chesterton, IN 46304

219-926-5781

EMAIL
graygoose@verizon.net

URL
www.graygooseinn.
com

GRAY GOOSE INN
Lite as a Cloud Pancakes

1⅓ cups cottage cheese	*2 Tbsp. melted butter*
3 eggs lightly beaten	*6 Tbsp. milk*
3 Tbsp. sugar	*1 cup flour*
2 tsp. lemon juice	*1 tsp. baking powder*
1 Tbsp. lemon zest	*1 dash salt*

Mix first 7 ingredients until smooth, stir in last 3 ingredients until just blended. Add 1 or 2 more tablespoons of milk if necessary to make a thinner batter. Cook over medium heat. Do not cook with too high of heat or pancakes will toughen.

   Serve with raspberry syrup, garnish with fresh raspberries, sprinkle with powdered sugar.

Yield: 6 servings

THE   BARN   INN

Barn Inn Oatmeal Pancakes

THE BARN INN

6838 CR 203
Millersburg, OH 44654

330-674-7600

EMAIL
reservations@
thebarninn.com

URL
www.thebarninn.com

4 cups uncooked rolled oats
    (either old fashioned or
    quick)
½ cup butter, melted
4 cups buttermilk
4 eggs, slightly beaten
1 cup milk

⅓ cup sugar
1 cup flour
2 teaspoons baking powder
2 teaspoons baking soda
1 teaspoon cinnamon
½ teaspoon salt
2 teaspoons butter flavoring

Combine rolled oats and melted butter in a bowl, then add all remaining ingredients. Cover and refrigerate several hours or overnight. If too thick, additional buttermilk or milk may be added. Fry on a griddle as usual.

   Serves 15 people. This recipe freezes very well and is requested almost every time I serve them.

Yield: 15 servings

Wood violets

THE WILDFLOWER
INN

PO Box 11000
Jackson, WY 83002

307-733-4710

EMAIL
jhwildflowerinn@
cs.com

URL
www.
jacksonholewildflower.
com

THE WILDFLOWER INN
Fantastic Buttermilk Pancakes

1 egg	*1 tsp baking soda*
1 cup buttermilk	*1 cup flour*
1 cup sour cream	
1 tsp baking powder	

The lightest, most delicious buttermilk pancakes ever!

Mix all ingredients together gently. Let sit for 10 minutes while the batter rises—very important. Lightly oil a medium hot grill. Use a ¼ cup measuring cup to pour out batter for pancakes.

Yield: 2 servings

THE ICE PALACE INN

Palace Puff Pancake

THE ICE PALACE INN

813 Spruce St
Leadville, CO 80461

719-486-8272

EMAIL
stay@icepalaceinn.com

URL
www.icepalaceinn.com

2 to 4 tbsp butter
¾ cup flour
½ cup of milk
½ cup heavy cream
1 tsp salt
1 tsp vanilla
4 eggs
⅛ teaspoon of baking powder
1 cup of blueberries or other fruit (if using apples or pears add 1 tsp
    of cinnamon and 2 tblsp of brown sugar)
¼ cup of sugar (if using apples or pear omit 2 tblsp)
confectioners sugar

Preheat oven to 400. Place cast iron skillet in oven to heat. Beat eggs, milk and cream until frothy, add vanilla, salt and flour beat until bubbly. When skillet is preheated place butter in and swirl around to coat bottom and sides.

Place a handfull of fruit in the bottom and sprinkle with about ¼ of the sugar. Place in oven for 1–2 minutes just until juices start to flow. Pour batter over fruit and sprinkle remaining fruit and sugar on top.

Place in oven for 20–25 minutes until puffed and golden. Let cool about 5 minutes before serving, sprinkle with confectioners sugar. Serve with warm maple syrup and sausage links.

Yield: 6 to 8 servings

THE DARBY FIELD INN

185 Chase Hill Rd
Albany, NH 03818

603-447-2181

EMAIL
marc@darbyfield.com

URL
www.darbyfield.com

THE DARBY FIELD INN

Heavenly Hots

4 whole eggs
½ tsp. salt
1½ tsp. baking soda
½ cup white flour
2 Tbsp. sugar

2 cups sour cream
½ tsp. nutmeg (optional)

Put all ingredients in a blender in the order in which they are listed and blend for 30 seconds. Wipe down the sides with a rubber spatula and blend again. Let set for 2–3 minutes, then pour on a hot griddle or a heavy weight frying pan in 3–4 inch circles. Flip them over when bubbles appear on the top and brown the other side.

These are great with pure maple syrup!

Yield: 6 servings

MAYOR'S MANSION INN

Cocoa Pancakes with Caramel Banana Topping

MAYOR'S MANSION
INN

801 Vine St
Chattanooga, TN 37403

423-265-5000

EMAIL
info@
mayorsmansioninn.com

URL
www.
mayorsmansioninn.com

Pancakes:
2 eggs
1 ½ cups milk
2 tablespoons oil
2 cups flour
½ cup sugar
4 tablespoons cocoa
2 teaspoons baking powder

Topping:
¾ cup packed brown sugar
½ cup heavy whipping cream
2 tablespoons vanilla
2 large bananas, sliced
*   diagonally*

Beat eggs until foamy. Beat in milk and oil. Add remaining pancake ingredients. Spoon batter onto hot griddle. Cook on both sides until golden brown.

For Topping:

Mix all ingredients except bananas in a saucepan. Heat gently to boiling over medium heat while stirring occasionally. Remove from heat and stir in bananas until coated.

INN AT THE
CROSSROADS

PO Box 6519
Charlottesville, VA
22906

434-979-6452

EMAIL
info@crossroadsinn.
com

URL
www.crossroadsinn.
com

INN AT THE CROSSROADS
Iron Skillet Baked Apple Pancake

3 tablespoons unsalted butter
2 large firm apples, peeled,
   cored and sliced to ¼ inch
   thickness
3 eggs
1 teaspoon granulated sugar

¼ cup (packed) light brown
   sugar
Pinch of salt
½ cup milk
½ cup all-purpose flour
¼ teaspoon ground cinnamon

Heat the oven to 450 degrees. Gently melt 2 tablespoons butter in a large (12 inch) ovenproof skillet. Add the apple slices and heat until tender, about 8–10 minutes.

Add 2 tablespoons of the brown sugar and stir to combine; remove from heat. Whisk the eggs, granulalted sugar, salt, milk and flour together in a bowl and then pour the mixture over the apples in the skillet.

Bake in the oven until puffy, about 10 minutes. While the skillet is in the oven, mix the cinnamon and the remaining brown sugar together.

Cut the remaining tablespoon of butter into small chunks. When the pancake puffs, remove it from the oven, dot it with butter, sprinkle with the cinnamon/brown sugar mixture and return to the oven until browned, about 10 more minutes.

Let set for 5 minutes and serve.

Yield: 4 servings

OLD HARBOR INN

Sour Cream Coffee Cake Grandmere

OLD HARBOR INN

22 Old Harbor Rd
Chatham, MA 02633

508-945-4434

EMAIL
info@
chathamoldharborinn.
com

URL
www.
chathamoldharborinn.
com

½ cup butter
1 cup sugar
2 eggs
2 cups all purpose flour
1 teaspoon vanilla
1 teaspoon baking soda
1 teaspoon baking powder
½ teaspoon salt
1 cup sour cream

Cream the butter until soft, then add the sugar and sour cream until light and fluffy. Add the eggs, one at a time, beating well after each addition. Sift the dry ingredients together.

Add the dry ingredients to the creamed mixture, alternating with the sour cream, beginning and ending with the flour mixture. Stir in the vanilla.

Pour half the batter into a well buttered 9 × 13 inch pan, cover with half of the nut filling (see below) pour the remaining batter over the filling and top with the remainder of the nut mixture. Bake at 325 for about 40 minutes.

Yield: 16 servings

Cooking Time: 30 min.

WILLOW SPRINGS
CABINS

11515 Sheridan Lake Rd
Rapid City, SD 57702

605-342-3665

EMAIL
wilosprs@rapidnet.com

URL
www.
willowspringscabins.
com

WILLOW SPRINGS CABINS

Raised Waffles

1 package yeast
½ cup warm water
2 cups milk, warmed
½ cup butter, melted
¼ teaspoon salt
2 teaspoons sugar
2 cups flour
2 eggs, beaten
¼ teaspoon baking soda

Dissolve the yeast in the warm water in a large bowl; let stand 5 minutes. Add the milk, butter, salt, sugar and flour to the yeast and beat until smooth. Cover bowl with plastic wrap and let sit at room temperature overnight. Batter can be kept in refrigerator for several days.

In the morning before cooking the waffles, add the eggs and baking soda, stirring till well mixed. The batter is thin. Pour ½ cup batter into a hot greased waffle iron.

Bake the waffles until there is no steam escaping from the waffle iron and the waffles are crisp. Serve at once.

Variations: Add chopped pecans or fresh coconut and serve with fresh fruit sauce.

Yield: 8 servings

JEWELED TURRET INN

Sourdough Gingerbread Belgium Waffles

JEWELED TURRET INN

40 Pearl St
Belfast, ME 04915

207-338-2304

EMAIL
info@jeweledturret.com

URL
www.jeweledturret.com

3 cups unbleached flour
3 tsp. baking powder
¾ tsp. baking soda
1½ tsp. salt
3 oz. sugar
¾ tsp. ground cinnamon

1½ tsp. ground ginger
3 eggs
¾ cup sourdough starter
¾ cup molasses
9 Tbsp. (½ cup) canola oil
1½ cups milk

In large glass or plastic bowl combine all dry ingredients. In medium (glass or plastic) bowl mix together wet ingredients using a plastic spatula or wooden spoon. Mix wet ingredients into dry ingredients just until moistened. Preheat waffle iron and oil each side with pastry brush. Pour batter onto iron and cook until golden brown. Sprinkle with confectioners sugar and top with fresh whipped cream. Makes 5 large waffles.

Sourdough Starter:
1 Tbsp. active dry yeast (1 envelope)
2½ cups warm water (105°F / 40°C)
2 Tbsp. honey
2½ cups unbleached flour

In 2-quart plastic juice pitcher with strainer lid mix yeast with water, then add honey and gradually stir in flour (use plastic spatula-no metal). Put strainer lid to open, so inside container will have air. Leave out overnight in warm place. The next morning mix ingredients with spatula and return lid to strainer position. Refrigerate and use as needed. Keeps approximately 10 days. To keep sourdough indefinately, every 7–10 days add equal parts flour and warm water- occasionally honey. Keep out overnight and again return to refrigerator the next day.

Tea Breads & Coffee Cakes

Tea breads and coffee cakes most typically are enjoyed in the afternoon hours as a light snack that provides an opportunity for everyone to gather and mingle for some time. Innkeepers often bake these breads themselves and truly enjoy offering their guests an occasion to sit down together and talk about their day. It is during these lingering afternoon hours munching on baked goods that innkeepers and guests form lasting friendships. But these tasty baked goods are not restricted to just afternoon snacking. Why not pair a nutty banana bread with a savory cup of joe to fuel you through your morning? If you find yourself needing a quick pick-me-up in the late morning or afternoon, reach for a piece of moist and crumbly coffee cake. Sift through the following recipes and you will see just how diverse these breads can be.

THE GLYNN HOUSE INN

Triple Chocolate Muffins

THE GLYNN HOUSE
INN

PO Box 719
Ashland, NH 03217

603-968-3775

EMAIL
innkeeper@glynnhouse.
com

URL
www.glynnhouse.com

1½ cups All Purpose Flour
1 tsp. Baking Powder
¼ cup Dutch Cocoa
½ tsp. salt
¼ cup butter
½ cup granulated sugar

1 egg
¾ cup milk
½ tsp. vanilla
½ cup chocolate chips
¼ cup white chocolate chips

Put flour, baking powder, salt and cocoa in a large bowl. Stir together making a well in the center. Beat butter, sugar and egg together well. Mix in milk and vanilla. Pour into the well and stir to moisten. Fold in the two types of chocolate chips. Do not over mix.

Bake in 400 F oven for 15 to 18 minutes. Use a wooden skewer to test the center of the muffin to ensure they are done.

Yield: 8 servings

Cooking Time: 30 min.

INN AT LOWER FARM

119 Mystic Rd
North Stonington, CT
06359

860-535-9075

EMAIL
info@lowerfarm.com

URL
www.lowerfarm.com

INN   AT   LOWER   FARM

Inn at Lower Farm Lemon Blueberry Biscuits

2 cups of all purpose flour
⅓ cup sugar
2 teaspoons of baking powder
½ teaspoon of baking soda
¼ teaspoon of salt

1 8-oz carton of lemon yogurt
1 egg lightly beaten
¼ cup melted butter
1 cup fresh or frozen blueberries

In a large bowl combine the dry ingredients. Combine the yogurt, egg and butter in a small bowl, stir into the dry ingredients just until moistened. Fold in the blueberries. Drop by spoonfuls onto a lightly greased baking sheet. Bake at 400 degrees for 15–18 minutes.

Yield: 1 dozen

Cooking Time: 30 min.

AVENUE INN B&B

Louisiana Cheddar Biscuit Ya Ya's

AVENUE INN B&B

4125 St Charles Ave
New Orleans, LA 70115

504-269-2640

EMAIL
stay@avenueinnbb.com

URL
www.avenueinnbb.com

2 cups self-rising sifted flour
¼ cup shortening
⅓ cup grated cheddar cheese
¼ teaspoon Chef Paul Prudhommes Vegetable Magic Seasoning
¾ cup milk

Heat oven to 450 degrees. In a large bowl add flour, cheese and seasoning, mix well. Cut shortening into dry ingredients until mixture resembles coarse crumbs. With a fork, stir in enough milk to form a soft dough or until dough pulls away from the sides of the bowl.

Turn dough onto lightly floured board or pastry cloth; knead just until smooth. Roll dough to ½ inch thickness; cut with floured 2-inch round cutter (a correct sized juice glass will do in a pinch). Place biscuits, just touching each other on an ungreased baking sheet (a little cooking spray wouldn't hurt, however). Bake at 450 degrees for 10–12 minutes or until golden brown.

Total preparation time: 20 minutes

Yield: 1 dozen

9E RANCH B&B

Smithville, TX 78957

512-497-9502

EMAIL
logcabins@9eranch.com

URL
www.9eranch.com

9 E   R A N C H   B & B

9E Ranch Biscuits

2 cups all purpose flour
2 tsp baking powder
½ tsp salt

¾ cup shredded cheddar cheese
½ cup shortening
1 cup buttermilk

In a bowl, combine flour, baking powder, baking soda and salt. Cut in cheese and shortening until crumbly. Add buttermilk; stir just until moistened. Turn onto a lightly floured surface, knead 8–10 times. roll out to ½ inch thickness; cut with a 2½ inch biscuit cutter. Place on an ungreased baking sheet. Bake at 435 degrees for 10 to 12 minutes or until golden brown.

*Great for a morning trail ride!

Yield: 16 biscuits

EL FAROLITO

Bonnie's Lemon Mango Ginger Bread

Batter:
1½ cups all-purpose flour
1 teaspoon baking powder
½ teaspoon baking soda
1¼ cups sugar
½ cup butter
3 eggs

½ cup lemon juice
⅛ teaspoon lemon extract
½ teaspoon powdered ginger
1 tablespoon crystallized
   ginger, finely chopped
¾ cup mango, diced and
   drained

Streusel:
½ cup pecans, finely chopped
¼ cup brown sugar
½ teaspoon nutmeg

In a medium bowl, stir together the flour, baking powder and baking soda.

In another bowl, with an electric mixer, beat butter and sugar until creamy. Then add eggs one at a time. Beat until fluffy. Beat in lemon juice and lemon extract, followed by milk, powdered ginger, and crystallized ginger.

Add slowly to dry ingredients. Stir in mangoes. Set aside.

Stir together streusel ingredients. Spoon ½ of the batter into a well greased 9 × 5 inch loaf pan. Sprinkle with ½ of the streusel. Spoon in remaining batter and top with the rest of the streusel.

Bake at 350 degrees for 50 to 60 minutes, or until a toothpick inserted in the center comes out clean. Cool before slicing. Makes one 9 × 5 loaf

Yield: 1 loaf

EL FAROLITO

514 Galisteo St
Santa Fe, NM 87501

505-988-1631

EMAIL
innkeeper@farolito.com

URL
www.farolito.com/

BISHOPSGATE INN

PO Box 290
East Haddam, CT 06423

860-873-1677

EMAIL
ctkagel@Bishopsgate.
com

URL
www.bishopsgate.com

BISHOPSGATE INN
New England Spiced Pumpkin Bread

3½ cups flour
2 teaspoons soda
2 teaspoons cinnamon
1 teaspoon salt
1 teaspoon nutmeg
½ teaspoon each of ginger and
    cloves

1 cup oil
2 cups sugar
4 eggs
2 cups pumpkin puree (or one
    can)
1 can frozen orange pineapple
    juice, thawed

Mix together dry ingredients. Add remaining ingredients.
    Pour into two oiled loaf pans. Bake at 350° for 65 minutes.
    Immediately pour orange pineapple juice over loaves and allow to soak in.

Yield: 2 loaves

BED   BREAKFAST   &
BEACH   IN   HANALEI

Carolyn's Best Banana Bread

*6 large, over ripe bananas,
    mashed*
4 eggs, well beaten
1 cub margarine or butter
½ cup oil
2 cups sugar
¼ cup lime or lemon juice

2 cups sifted flour
2 tsp baking soda
1 tsp salt
1 cup chopped walnuts
*2 to 3 Tbsp grated lemon or
    lime peel*

Beat bananas, add eggs and set aside. Cream margarine and oil with sugar until fluffy. Add banana mixture and juice; blend well. Add flour, soda and salt; stir until smooth. Fold in walnuts and peel. Pour into 2 well greased and floured 9 × 5 loaf pans. Bake at 350 degrees for 40–45 minutes.

*This recipe turns out best if you take bread out of the oven slightly under-baked.

Yield: 2 loaves

BED BREAKFAST &
BEACH IN HANALEI

PO Box 748
Hanalei, HI 96714

808-826-6111

EMAIL
hanaleibay@aol.com

URL
www.
bestvacationinparadise.
com/bandb.htm

INN BY THE MILL

1679 Mill Rd
St. Johnsville, NY 13452

518-568-2388

EMAIL
stay@innbythemill.com

URL
www.innbythemill.com

INN BY THE MILL
Grist Mill Banana Bread

½ cup butter
1 cup sugar
2 eggs
1½ cups mashed bananas
   (about 3 large bananas)
1 tsp vanilla

2 Tbsp sour cream
2 cups flour
1 tsp baking powder
1 tsp salt
½ tsp baking soda
1 cup chopped nuts

Cream butter and sugar. Add eggs one at a time. Beat in at low speed, the mashed banana, sour cream and vanilla. Mix together all the dry ingredients. Add to banana mixture. Fold in nuts.

   Bake in greased loaf pan, bundt pan or fluted pan at 350 degrees for 45 to 55 minutes depending on the size of the pan. You may also bake in mini loaves, just adjust the baking time.

Happy Baking!

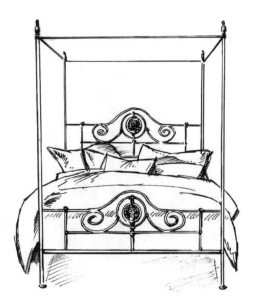

MAGNOLIA PLANTATION

Tropical Pumpkin Bread

2 cups sugar
5 eggs
1½ cups oil
2 cups canned pumpkin
3 cups flour
2 tsp soda

1 tsp cinnamon
1 tsp salt
2 packages instant coconut
    pudding mix
1 cup chopped nuts, any kind

In a medium bowl, mix together first four ingredients. Stir in flour, soda, cinnamon and salt. Blend in pudding mix and stir in nuts. Pour into 2 loaf pans. Bake in 350 degree oven for 45 minutes or until toothpick inserted in center comes out clean.

MAGNOLIA
PLANTATION

309 SE 7th St
Gainesville, FL 32601

352-375-6653

EMAIL
info@magnoliabnb.com

URL
www.magnoliabnb.com

HEARTHSTONE
ELEGANT LODGE BY
THE RIVER

PO Box 1492
Kamiah, ID 83536

208-935-1492

EMAIL
visit@hearthstone-lodge.com

URL
www.hearthstonelodge.com

HEARTHSTONE ELEGANT LODGE BY THE RIVER

Hearthstone's Delicious Lemon Bread

6 tablespoons butter, softened
1 cup sugar
2 eggs
1½ cups flour
1¼ teaspoons baking powder
½ teaspoon salt
½ cup milk
½ cup chopped pecans
¼ cup powdered sugar
Rind & juice from one lemon

Beat butter and sugar until fluffy. Add eggs, beat, and set aside. Combine flour, baking powder & salt. Add to butter/sugar mixture gradually, alternating with ½ cup milk. Add chopped pecans & lemon rind. Pour into a loaf pan. Bake 1 hour at 325 degrees.

Remove from oven and immediately pour lemon juice over loaf. Then sprinkle ¼ cup powdered sugar over loaf.

Let cool and then remove from pan.

Yield: 1 loaf

A L O D G E   A T   S E D O N A
- A   L U X U R Y   B & B   I N N

Pear, Walnut and Blue Cheese Flat bread

Dough:
1 tablespoon dry active yeast
1 ½ cups warm water
3 cups All Purpose flour
2 teaspoons sugar
½ tablespoon salt
½ cup chopped walnuts
2 tablespoons olive oil
1 large egg

Topping:
2 cups pears pureed
3 ounce blue cheese crumbles
½ cup walnuts
1 cup jack cheese
1 tablespoon chopped rosemary

A LODGE AT SEDONA -
A LUXURY B&B INN

125 Kallof Pl
Sedona, AZ 86336

928-204-1942

EMAIL
Info@
LODGEatSEDONA.
com

URL
www.
LODGEatSEDONA.
com

Preheat oven to 450°F.

Dough:
Mix yeast, 1 teaspoon sugar and water together and set aside. Put flour, ½ tablespoon, salt, 2 teaspoons sugar, walnuts and olive oil in food processor and mix. When yeast has foam on top, add to food processor and process until it comes together. This is enough kneading. Put dough in a well-oiled bowl and cover with plastic wrap. Allow to rise for 1 hour. Prepare a full sheet pan with Pam, oil spray, and sprinkle with corn meal. Press dough on pan.

Toppings:
Spread pear puree on dough. Top with cheeses, walnuts and rosemary. Bake for 15 minutes or until the cheeses have melted and browned slightly.

Garnish and Presentation:
Cut flat bread in 1″ × 1″ squares and serve on a platter. Can be served with herbed olive oil or a stilton and garlic spread.

Cooking Time: 30 min.

WHITEGATE INN BY
THE SEA

PO Box 150
Mendocino, CA 95460

707-937-4892

EMAIL
staff@whitegateinn.com

URL
www.whitegateinn.
com/whitegate.php

WHITEGATE INN BY THE SEA

Spicy Pineapple Zucchini Bread

3 eggs
1 cup salad oil
2½ cups sugar
2 teaspoons vanilla
2 cups coarsely shredded, unpeeled zucchini (about 2 medium)
1 can (8¼ ounce) well-drained, crushed pineapple

3 cups all-purpose flour, unsifted (half of which can be whole wheat)
2 teaspoons soda
1 teaspoon salt
½ teaspoon baking powder
1½ teaspoons ground cinnamon
¾ teaspoon ground nutmeg
1 cup chopped walnuts (finely)

In a large bowl, beat eggs until frothy. Add oil, sugar and vanilla. Continue beating until mixture is thick and foamy.

Stir in zucchini and pineapple (gently).

In a separate bowl, stir together flour, soda, salt, baking powder, cinnamon, nutmeg and walnuts. Stir gently into zucchini mixture until just blended.

Spoon batter into 2 greased and flour-dusted loaf pans.

Bake in a 350° oven for 1 hour or until a wooden toothpick inserted in the centers come out clean.

Let cool in pans 10 minutes, then turn out onto racks to cool completely. Enjoy!

Yield: 2 loaves

INN AT MONTICELLO
Chocolate Zucchini Rum Coffee Cake

INN AT MONTICELLO

1188 Scottsville Rd
Charlottesville, VA
22902

434-979-3593

EMAIL
stay@innatmonticello.
com

URL
www.innatmonticello.
com

1½ sticks butter at room
    temperature
2 cups sugar
3 large eggs
2½ cups flour
½ cup unsweetened cocoa
1½ tsp baking soda

1 tsp salt
1 tsp cinnamon
¼ cup milk
⅓ cup rum
3 cups shredded zucchini
1 cup chocolate chips
½ cup chopped pecans

In large bowl, beat sugar and butter until fluffy. Add eggs, one at a time. Add flour, cocoa, soda, salt, cinnamon, milk and rum. Beat until well mixed. Add zucchini, chocolate and nuts, again mixing well.

Pour into sprayed bundt pan. Bake in 350 degree oven, 50–55 minutes.

HENRY FARM INN

2206 Green Mountain
Tpke
Chester, VT 05143

802-875-2674

EMAIL
info@henryfarminn.
com

URL
www.henryfarminn.
com

HENRY FARM INN
Sour Cream Coffee Cake

Coffee Cake:
1 cup butter, softened
1½ cups sugar
3 eggs
1 teaspoon vanilla
3 cups all-purpose flour
2½ teaspoons baking powder
1 teaspoon salt
¼ teaspoon baking soda
1 cup sour cream
½ cup milk

Filling:
¼ cup firmly packed brown
*   sugar*
1 teaspoon cinnamon
½ cup chopped pecans

Heat oven to 350 degrees. Grease and flour 10-inch tube pan. In large bowl, combine butter and sugar; beat until light and fluffy. Add eggs one at a time, beating well after each addition. Add vanilla; blend well. In a large bowl, combine flour, baking powder, salt and baking soda; mix well. Alternately add flour mixture, sour cream and milk to butter mixture, beginning and ending with flour mixture and mixing well after each addition. Spoon half of batter into greased and floured pan. In small bowl, combine all filling ingredients; mix well. Sprinkle mixture evenly over batter in pan. Spoon remaining batter over filling.

Bake at 350 degrees F for 50–60 minutes or until toothpick inserted 1 inch from edge comes out clean. Cool in pan 10 minutes; invert onto wire rack. Cool at least 15 minutes. Serve warm or cool.

Yield: 15 servings

BLUE   BELLE   INN

Raspberry or Blueberry Streusel Coffee Cake

BLUE BELLE INN

PO Box 205
St. Ansgar, IA 50472
641-713-3113
EMAIL
bluebelle@omnitelcom.
com
URL
www.BlueBelleInn.com

2 cups all-purpose flour
¾ cup sugar
2½ teaspoons baking powder
¾ teaspoon salt
¼ cup shortening
¾ cup milk
1 egg
1-2 cups well drained berries

Heat oven to 325°F. Grease round layer pan 9 × 1½ inch or square pan, 8 × 8x2 or 9 × 9x2 inch. Blend all ingredients except topping and blueberries or raspberries; beat vigorously ½ minute. Fold in berries. Spread in pan. Sprinkle topping over batter and use a fork to poke and twist topping down into batter. Bake 25–30 min or until wooden pick inserted in center comes out clean. Serves 8–12.

Streusel Topping: Mix ⅔ cup brown sugar (packed), ½ cup flour, 1 teaspoon cinnamon and 6 tablespoons firm butter until crumbly.

Raspberry Sauce (to be served on the side or drizzled on top): In a food processor or blender, process 1 (10 ounce) package frozen raspberries in syrup, thawed, with syrup, until smooth. If desired strain to remove seeds. In small saucepan, combine 3 tablespoons sugar and 1 teaspoon cornstarch; stir in raspberry puree. Cook and stir on medium heat until it boils and thickens. Cool to room temperature.

Cooking Time: 30 min.

QUINTESSENTIALS
B&B & SPA

PO Box 574
East Marion, NY 11939

631-477-9400

EMAIL
innkeeper@
quintessentialsinc.com

URL
www.
QuintessentialsInc.com

QUINTESSENTIALS B & B & SPA

Jalepeno Corn Kernel Cheddar Muffins

1 cup (8 oz) all-purpose flour
1 cup (8 oz) cornmeal, yellow
    or white
3 tablespoons sugar
1 tablespoon baking powder
½ teaspoon salt
1 cup (8 fl oz) milk
1 egg

½ cup fresh corn kernels or
    thawed frozen corn kernels
½ cup grated cheddar cheese
1 tablespoon fresh jalapeno
    pepper diced small or
    bottled jalapeno pepper
¼ cup (2 oz) unsalted butter
    melted

Pre-heat oven to 400 degrees F. Butter or spray oil in standard muffin tins.

In medium bowl stir and toss together the flour, cornmeal, sugar, baking powder and salt. Set aside.

In a small bowl whisk together the milk, egg, corn kernels, cheddar and jalapeno until blended. Add the melted butter. Combine wet and dry ingredients, and stir just until blended.

Spoon into the prepared muffin tins, filling each cup about two-thirds full. Bake until a toothpick inserted in the center of a muffin comes out clean, about 15 minutes.

Cool in the tins for 5 minutes, then, remove.

Yield: 1 dozen

MOSTLY HALL

Cheese Blintz Muffins

MOSTLY HALL

27 Main St
Falmouth, MA 02540

508-548-3786

EMAIL
stay@mostlyhall.com

URL
www.mostlyhall.com

1 lb ricotta cheese
3 eggs
2 Tbsp sour cream or yogurt
¼ cup melted butter

½ cup Bisquick
⅓ cup sugar

Preheat oven to 350. Mix all ingredients together and spoon into greased muffin tin. Bake for 30 minutes until lightly browned. Place two muffins on each plate and spoon over Blueberry Sauce. Top with a dollop of sour cream.

Blueberry Sauce
Combine 1 Tbsp cornstarch with ⅓ cup warm water to disolve lumps. Add ⅓ cup sugar, 2 Tbsp lemon juice and 2 cups fresh or frozen blueberries. Cook over medium heat, stirring until mixture is thickened. Makes about 2 cups sauce.

GREENFIELD INN

PO Box 400
Greenfield, NH 03047

603-547-6327

EMAIL
innkeeper@
greenfieldinn.com

URL
www.greenfieldinn.com

GREENFIELD INN
Heavenly Muffins

2 cups bran
1 cup oatmeal
2½ cups flour
2 tbsp plus 2 tsp baking powder
2 tsp baking soda
2 tsp cinnamon
1½ tsp. cloves
1 tsp. salt
3 cups walnuts (chopped)
2 cups dark raisins
1 cup yellow raisins
1 cup butter
1½ cups molasses
4 eggs
2 cups milk soured with 2 tbsp. vinegar

Plump raisins in water for a few minutes and drain. Combine all dry ingredients, drained raisins, and walnuts. Combine cold butter and flour in food processor. Process to a mealy texture. Beat eggs, milk, and molasses together. Combine wet and dry ingredients. Mound into paper-lined muffin tins. Sprinkle with raw sesame and sunflower seeds.

Bake in a 375 degree oven for approximately 20 minutes.

Yield: 2 dozen

A N G E L   O F   T H E   S E A
Streusel Raspberry Muffins

ANGEL OF THE SEA

5 Trenton Ave
Cape May, NJ 08204

609-884-3369

EMAIL
info@angelofthesea.com

URL
www.angelofthesea.
com

1½ cups flour
2 tsp baking powder
½ cup butter, melted
1½ cups fresh raspberries
½ cup sugar
½ cup milk
1 egg

Topping:
¼ cup walnuts, chopped
¼ cup flour
¼ cup brown sugar
2 Tbsp butter, melted

Preheat oven to 400 degrees. In a large bowl, mix flour, sugar and baking powder. In a smaller bowl combine milk, butter and egg, stir into the dry ingredients and mix until moist. Spoon half of the batter into greased and floured muffin pans.

Divide raspberries evenly in muffin pans. Top each with the remaining batter. Thoroughly mix together the topping ingredients. Sprinkle the crumb topping evenly on top and bake 25–30 minutes.

Delicious served warm.

Yield: 1 dozen

Cooking Time: 30 min.

WHITE FENCE B&B

275 Chapel Rd
Stanley, VA 22851

540-778-4680

EMAIL
cwilliams@cox.net

URL
www.whitefencebb.
com

WHITE   FENCE   B & B

Sour Cream Coffeecake Muffins

Filling:
½ cup brown sugar
½ cup finely chopped walnuts
1 teaspoon ground cinnamon

Muffins:
½ cup butter
½ cup sugar
2 eggs
1 cup sour cream

1 teaspoon vanilla
2 cups all purpose flour
1 teaspoon baking powder
1 teaspoon baking soda
¼ teaspoon salt

Preheat oven to 375°F. Grease muffin tins.

Mix butter, sugar and eggs. Add sour cream and vanilla. Add dry ingredients. Sprinkle filling mix (except for 2 tablespoons) on top of batter and cut through the batter with a knife to marble with filling.

Spoon batter into 12 greased regular sized muffins cups. Sprinkle tops with remaining filling. Bake 22 minutes. Remove from pan and cool.

Yield: 1 dozen

HOMESTEAD LODGING

Lemon Raspberry Streusel Muffins

2 cups flour
½ cup sugar
2 teaspoons baking powder
½ teaspoon baking soda
½ teaspoon salt
8 ounces lemon yogurt
½ cup oil
1 teaspoon grated lemon peel
2 eggs
l cup fresh or frozen raspberries,
    thawed

TOPPING
⅓ cup sugar
¼ cup flour
2 tablespoons margarine or
    butter

Preheat oven to 400°F. Grease 36 mini muffin cups.

In a large bowl, combine flour, sugar, baking powder, baking soda, and salt; mix well.

In small bowl, combine yogurt, oil, lemon peels and eggs; mix well. Add to dry ingredients; stir until dry ingredients are moistened. Gently stir in rasberries.

Fill greased muffin cups ¾ full. For the topping, combine the ⅓ c sugar and ⅓ c flour in a small bowl. Using a pastry blender or fork, cut in margarine until crumbly. Sprinkle over batter.

Bake at 400°F for 11–13 minutes or until light brown and toothpick inserted in center comes out clean. Cool 5 minutes; remove from muffin cups. Serve warm.

Yield: 3 dozen

HOMESTEAD
LODGING

184 Eastbrook Rd
Smoketown, PA 17576

717-393-6927

EMAIL
lkepiro@comcast.net

URL
www.
homesteadlodging.net

WHITE LACE INN

16 N 5th Ave
Sturgeon Bay, WI 54235

920-743-1105

EMAIL
Romance@
WhiteLaceInn.com

URL
www.whitelaceinn.com

W H I T E   L A C E   I N N
Door County Cherry Muffins

4 cups flour
2 cups sugar
2 tbsp. baking powder
1 tsp. cinnamon
3 cups frozen & rinsed Door
    County cherries
1 cup butter (melted)
1 cup milk
4 eggs
1 tsp. vanilla

Topping:
1 cup flour
⅓ cup soft butter
½ cup sugar
½ tsp. cinnamon

Preheat oven to 425°F. Combine dry ingredients and blend. In a separate bowl, toss 1 tbsp. of dry ingredients with cherries. In a large bowl, mix butter, milk, eggs and vanilla. Then add dry ingredients and stir until well moistened. Stir in cherries. Spoon batter into muffin tins to about ¾ full and sprinkle with topping mixture. Bake at 425°F for 15–20 minutes.

Optional topping — sprinkle with sugar.

Yield: 2 dozen

AMERICUS GARDEN INN

Chocolate Ricotta Muffins

AMERICUS GARDEN
INN

504 Rees Pk
Americus, GA 31709

229-931-0122

EMAIL
info@
americusgardeninn.com

URL
www.
americusgardeninn.com

2⅓ cups flour
1 cup sugar
¾ cup semisweet chocolate chips
⅓ cup cocoa
2 teaspoons baking powder
¾ teaspoon salt
1 cup ricotta cheese
2 large eggs, lightly beaten
1⅓ cups milk
1 teaspoon vanilla
¼ cup canola oil
Cooking spray

Preheat oven to 350°F.

Spray ¼ cup muffin tins with cooking spray. In a large bowl, mix flour, sugar, chips, cocoa, baking powder and salt.

In a medium bowl mix cheese with eggs, one at a time, beating well after each addition. Whisk in milk and vanilla until blended. Fold cheese mixture and oil into flour mixture until just blended. Spoon batter into muffin cups.

Bake 25 minutes or until wooden pick inserted in center comes out clean. Remove from pans immediately and cool on a wire rack.

Yield: 18 servings

7 GABLES INN &
SUITES

PO Box 80488
Fairbanks, AK 99708

907-479-0751

EMAIL
gables7@alaska.net

URL
www.7gablesinn.com

7 GABLES INN & SUITES
Cappuccino Chip Muffins

Muffins:
2 cups flour
¾ cup sugar
2½ teaspoons baking powder
*2 teaspoons instant espresso
    coffee powder*
½ teaspoon salt
½ teaspoon ground cinnamon
1 cup milk, scalded and cooled
*½ cup sweet butter, melted and
    cooled*
1 egg, lightly beaten
1 teaspoon vanilla extract
*¾ cup semi-sweet chocolate
    mini chips*

Spread:
4 ounces cream cheese, softened
*1 square (1 ounce) semi-sweet
    chocolate, melted and
    cooled*
1 tablespoon sugar
½ teaspoon vanilla
*½ teaspoon instant espresso
    coffee powder*

Muffins:
Preheat oven to 375 degrees. Grease 12 four ounce or 6 eight ounce muffin tins. In a large bowl, stir together flour, sugar, baking powder, espresso coffee powder, salt, and cinnamon. In another medium bowl, stir together milk, butter, egg, and vanilla until blended. Make a well in center of dry ingredients, add milk mixture and stir just to combine. Stir in chips. Spoon batter into prepared muffin tins and bake 15–20 minutes or until top springs back when touched. Turn out muffins onto wire rack.

Spread:
Place cream cheese, chocolate, sugar, vanilla, and espresso powder in a small bowl and blend thoroughly until smooth and of a consistent color. To serve, allow 10 minutes to soften at room temperature. Serve muffins with a generous amount of Chocolate Espresso Cream Cheese Spread.

Yield: 1 dozen

EAGLES NEST INN

Lemon Huckleberry Muffins

3½ cups flour
1 cup granulated sugar
2 tsp baking powder
1 tsp baking soda
1 tsp salt
½ cup flaked coconut
½ cup wild Huckleberries, fresh
or frozen

2 tbsp lemon zest
2 cups buttermilk
2 eggs
6 tbsp vegetable oil, or melted
butter
1 tsp lemon flavoring, or lemon
oil

EAGLES NEST INN

4680 Saratoga Rd
Langley, WA 98260

360-221-5331

EMAIL
eaglnest@whidbey.com

URL
www.eaglesnestinn.
com

Preheat oven to 400 degrees. Measure all the dry ingredients and place in a large mixing bowl. Add the berries into dry mixture and coat with flour. In a separate bowl, place all of the liquid ingredients and blend with a whisk.

Make a well in the center of the dry ingredients and dump the liquid ingredients in all at once. Mix quickly and lightly just until all the ingredients are moistened. Do not over mix or muffins will be tough. Spoon into muffin tins lined with cups. Muffin cups will be full and pile high in the center. Bake in the center of the oven 20–25 minutes. Cool.

Yield: 1 dozen

MOONDANCE INN

1105 W 4th St
Red Wing, MN 55066

651-388-8145

EMAIL
info@moondanceinn.
com

URL
www.moondanceinn.
com

MOONDANCE INN
Harry's Scones

4 cups flour
⅔ cup sugar
2 tablespoons baking powder
12 teaspoons butter—cold
1 cup chopped walnuts
1 cup diced, dried apricots
    (hint: if too sticky; put in
    freezer for awhile—they'll
    be easier to dice)

1 cup white chocolate chips
2 eggs
1 cup heavy whipping cream
    (don't substitute half-and-
    half or milk—they won't
    turn out!)
2 teaspoon vanilla

Put the first 4 ingredients in food processor; process until it looks crumbly. If you don't have food processor, cut butter into dry stuff with 2 knives. Pour into bowl.

Gently mix in next 3 ingredients.

In a separate bowl, combine the last 3 ingredients, then pour the liquid into the dry stuff. Mix and form a huge gloppy ball; knead in all flour.

You can form the scones in 2 ways:

Pat about ¾ –1 inch thick. Cut into triangular wedges and place on cookie sheet.

Brush tops with a little heavy cream.

Bake at 350°F; about 18–20 minutes.

OLDE   WORLD   B & B
AND   TEA   ROOM

Cream Scones with Honey Butter

OLDE WORLD B&B
AND TEA ROOM

2982 State Rt 516 NW
Dover, OH 44622

330-343-1333

EMAIL
info@oldeworldbb.com

URL
www.oldeworldbb.com

2 cups flour
2 tablespoons sugar
1 tablespoon baking powder
⅓ cup chilled butter
1 cup whipping cream

Preheat oven to 350°F.

Spray baking sheet with nonstick cooking spray. Combine first 3 ingredients. Cut in chilled butter. Add whipping cream. Mix until moist. Knead 5–7 times, until a soft moist dough forms.

Divide into 3 equal portions. Pat each portion out to ½ inch thick, cut into 8 wedges and place on baking sheet. Repeat with other 2 portions.

Bake for 10–15 minutes or just until bottoms begin to brown.

Honey Butter:

Mix equal portions of butter (at room temperature) and honey. Mix well. Best served fresh.

For variation, add a complementary flavoring such as cinnamon, almond extract, herbs or nuts.

Yield: 2 dozen

FITZGERALD'S IRISH
B&B

47 Mentor Ave
Painesville, OH 44077

440-639-0845

EMAIL
fitzbb@gmail.com

URL
www.fitzgeraldbb.com

FITZGERALD'S IRISH B & B

Irish Raisin Scones

2 cups flour
2 teaspoons baking powder
¼ teaspoon salt
8 tablespoons cold unsalted butter
½ cup raisins covered in cinnamon
½ cup milk
1 egg
2 tablespoons sugar

Sift together 2 cups all-purpose flour, 2 teaspoons baking powder, 2 tablespoons sugar, and ¼ teaspoon salt in a large bowl. Cut 8 tablespoons (1 stick) butter into bits and, with your fingertips mix into flour mixture until it resembles coarse meal.

Using a fork, stir in ½ cup dark raisins, ½ cup milk, and egg until combined. Transfer to a lightly floured surface and, with floured hands, knead it until it forms a dough. Roll out dough into a 9 inch round (about ½ inch thick) and cut out scones with a 2½ inch round cutter.

Arrange scones 1 inch apart on a buttered large baking sheet and gently re-roll and cut out scraps.

Bake scones in middle of a 350 degrees F oven until pale golden, about 12–15 minutes, and transfer to a rack to cool.

Sprinkle with cinnamon and serve warm.

Yield: 12 servings

BUTTONWOOD INN

Buttonwood Inn Scones

BUTTONWOOD INN

50 Admiral Dr
Franklin, NC 28734

828-369-8985

EMAIL
info@buttonwoodbb.
com

URL
www.buttonwoodbb.
com

2 cups all-purpose flour
1½ tsp. baking powder
½ tsp. baking soda
¼ tsp. salt
⅓ cup sugar

Combine these ingredients.
Cut in 6 tbsp. butter (cold)
Combine 1 egg
½ cup buttermilk
1½ tsp. vanilla

Add to dry mixture and stir till all is well mixed. Drop by Tbsp. on parchment lined cookie sheet. Bake at 400 degrees for 12–15 minutes. Serve with butter and jam or Lemon Butter.

Lemon Butter:
1 stick butter
4 eggs
Pinch of salt

2 cups sugar
3 lemons (juice and peel)

Melt butter in top of double boiler. Beat eggs with pinch of salt. Beat in sugar slowly till dissolved and eggs are lemon colored (5–8 mins.) Add juice and peel. Beat several minutes. Cook and stir till thick. Store in glass jars in the refrigerator. Will keep for several weeks. Use on scones, muffins, coffeecakes, and to fill tart shells.

THE RED CASTLE INN
HISTORIC LODGINGS

109 Prospect St
Nevada City, CA 95959

530-265-5135

EMAIL
stay@redcastleinn.com

URL
www.redcastleinn.com

THE RED CASTLE INN
HISTORIC LODGINGS

Treacle Cake (Gingerbread)

2 cups all purpose flour, sifted
1 teaspoon baking soda
¼ teaspoon nutmeg
⅛ teaspoon cloves
1 teaspoon ginger

¼ teaspoon cinnamon
1 cup molasses
1 tablespoon honey
5 tablespoons soft butter
½ cup boiling water

Preheat the oven to 375°F. Butter a 9 × 9 inch square baking pan

In a large bowl, sift together the flour, baking soda and spices.

In another bowl, mix together the molasses, honey, butter, and boiling water. Working quickly, add the wet ingredients to the dry, combine well and pour into the prepared pan.

Bake for about 20 minutes or until a toothpick in the center comes out clean. Cut into 16 squares and serve warm in muffin papers.

Yield: 16 servings

Appetizers

Inns that follow the custom of beverages and hors d'oeuvres usually do so between 6:00 and 8:00 p.m. By that time, guests have had a chance to relax in their rooms and change into evening clothes, before congregating for a little conviviality prior to a night on the town.

The hors d'oeuvres dishes in this book will be interesting additions to your next party tray, where you'll be able to introduce your guests to some exciting new treats.

THE CHANEY MANOR
B&B INN

7864 Newark Rd
Mount Vernon, OH
43050

740-392-2304

EMAIL
chaney@ecr.net

URL
www.
thechaneymanorbandb.
com

THE CHANEY MANOR B&B INN

Brazil Nuts in Roasted Butter Glaze

Shelled whole Brazil Nuts
Butter (not margarine or substitute)
Brown sugar
Cinnamon

Melt 2 tablespoons of butter into frying pan. Add 1 cup of whole shelled Brazil nuts. Brown lightly for about 2–3 minutes over medium heat. Add brown sugar and a dash of cinnamon. Remove from heat and stir well.

Maximum prep. time: 5 minutes.

These can be placed in small nut cups, directly on the plate for accent, or as a topping for French toast.

Yield: 4 servings

Cooking Time: 5 min.

A L P E N H O R N   B & B
Spinach Balls Hors d'oeuvres

ALPENHORN B&B

PO Box 2912
Big Bear, CA 92315

909-866-5700

EMAIL
linda@alpenhorn.com

URL
www.alpenhorn.com/
welcome.html

Ingredients (for a double batch):
4 10-ounce boxes chopped frozen spinach, drained
4 cups of herbed bread crumbs, crushed
2 cups packed Parmesan cheese
1 cup melted butter
8 small green onions, chopped
6 eggs
Dash nutmeg

Mix all ingredients together. Form balls. Freeze. Before serving, bake at 350° for 10–15 minutes. Serve with sauce, below.

Sauce (cut ingredients in half for one recipe):
1 cup Grey Poupon mustard
1 cup honey
2 egg yolks

Mix honey and mustard, and then add egg yolk. Cook over low heat, stirring constantly, until slightly thickened.

   Cover and chill. Serve at room temperature or slightly warmed.

AMERICA'S ROCKY
MOUNTAIN LODGE &
CABINS

4680 Hagerman Ave
Cascade, CO 80809

719-684-2521

EMAIL
info@
rockymountainlodge.
com

URL
www.
rockymountainlodge.
com

AMERICA'S ROCKY MOUNTAIN LODGE & CABINS

Brie and Crab-Stuffed Mushrooms

18 large mushrooms, stems removed and chopped
2 tablespoons melted butter
1 teaspoon garlic salt
2 tablespoons minced onion
1 teaspoons Worcestershire sauce
4 oz jumbo lump crabmeat
1 tablespoon mayonnaise
3 oz Brie, cut in 18 pieces

Preheat oven to 350°F. Place mushroom caps on a cookie sheet. Brush caps with some of the butter and sprinkle with garlic salt.

In a skillet, sauté the mushroom stems with onion, Worcestershire sauce using the remaining butter.

In a bowl, mix crabmeat and mayonnaise. Fill caps with mushroom and onion mixture. Top with crabmeat and Brie. Bake for 10 minutes or until mushrooms are tender and cheese is melted.

Yield: 6 servings

ALBEMARLE INN

Eggplant and Goat Cheese Crostini

ALBEMARLE INN

86 Edgemont Rd
Asheville, NC 28801

828-255-0027

EMAIL
info@albemarleinn.com

URL
www.albemarleinn.com

1 Tbsp. olive oil
1 small medium eggplant, peeled and cut in a small dice
1 medium tomato, diced
1 yellow bell pepper, diced
1 red pepper, diced
¼ cup balsamic vinegar
1 garlic clove, minced
1 ½ tsp. cumin
1 Tbsp. finely chopped parsley
 ½ tsp. thyme
¼ tsp. cayenne pepper

Heat oil in a large skillet. Add eggplant, tomato, peppers, vinegar, garlic and cumin; bring to a boil.

Cover and cook over medium-low heat, stirring occasionally, until thickened (approx. 20–25 minutes).

Uncover and cook, stirring until liquid evaporates (approx. 2 minutes). Stir in parsley, thyme and cayenne. Let cool.

Spread toasted baguette with goat cheese and then dollop 1 Tbsp. eggplant spread on top.

WELCOME HOME B&B

PO Box 333
4260 W Hawthorne Dr
(Hwy Y)
Newburg, WI 53060

262-675-2525

EMAIL
welcomehome@hnet.
net

WELCOME HOME B&B

Baked Brie in Bread

*1 round or oval loaf of white,
    wheat or rye bread*
2 cloves garlic, minced

2 tablespoon butter, melted
1 to 2 pounds Brie cheese

With sharp knife, cut just inside outer edge of bread leaving a shell. Do not cut through bottom. Gently remove insides of bread creating a cavity for the cheese and cut into pieces for dipping. Mix garlic and butter. Paint inside of shell with mixture. Reserve remaining mixture. Trim cheese to fit inside shell, leaving rind on if desired. Place loaf on a baking sheet and bake at 350°F for 15–20 minutes or until cheese is melted. Spread remainng butter mixture on bread pieces. Place on a baking sheet and toast at 350°F oven for 10–15 minutes or until lightly browned. Use to dip in the cheese. Sliced fruit—grapes, apples and pears can also be used for dipping.

Yield: 10 servings

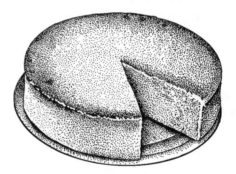

MADRONA MANOR WINE COUNTRY INN & RESTAURANT

California Seafood Cocktail

For Cocktail base:
2 cups fish broth or clam juice
¼ cup catsup
hot sauce to taste

To Serve:
4 calamari, cleaned, poached
4 scallops, cut in half, poached
*3 ounces salmon, cut ¼ inch
    cubes, poached*
*6 prawns (any size) cleaned,
    poached*
2 tablespoons red onions, diced

*1 tablespoon red bell pepper,
    diced*
¼ avocado, diced
1 tablespoon cilantro, chopped
Corn chips
Lemon wedges

Mix cocktail base ingredients thoroughly. Poach seafood in water.
Place seafood in a cold margarita glass and add vegetables. Pour
cocktail base over top of seafood and vegetables. Garnish plate
with corn chips and lemon wedges.

MADRONA MANOR
WINE COUNTRY INN
& RESTAURANT

1001 Westside Rd
Healdsburg, CA 95448

707-433-4231

EMAIL
info@madronamanor.
com

URL
www.madronamanor.
com

CASA SEDONA B&B
INN

55 Hozoni Dr
Sedona, AZ 86336

928-282-2938

EMAIL
casa@sedona.net

URL
www.casasedona.com

CASA SEDONA B&B INN

Hot Fiesta Spinach Dip

1 cup chopped onion
1 cup salsa
1 10-ounce package chopped
    spinach, thawed and
    squeezed dry
2½ cups grated Jack cheese

8 ounces cream cheese, cut into
    small cubes
½ cup sliced black olives
1 cup chopped pecans

Combine onion, salsa, spinach, 2 cups cheese, cream cheese and olives. Transfer to oven-proof serving dish and top with pecans.

Bake about 30 minutes at 400°F until hot and bubbly. Top with remaining cheese. Serve hot with corn chips.

COUNTRY LIFE B & B

Smoked Oyster Spread

COUNTRY LIFE B&B

67 Tabor Rd
Greenwich, NY 12834

518-692-7203

EMAIL
stay@countrylifebb.com

URL
www.countrylifebb.
com

1 8-oz package cream cheese
⅛ cup milk
1–2 Tbsp mayonnaise
½ Tbsp lemon juice

½ Tbsp worcestershire sauce
dash of Tabasco and salt
1 can smoked oysters, chopped
paprika and chopped parsley

Combine first 6 ingredients and blend well. Add oysters. Put into serving bowl, sprinkle with paprika and parsley.

Refrigerate several hours or overnight. Serve with mild crackers, like Towne House or Ritz.

HIGHLAND LODGE

1608 Craftsbury Rd
Greensboro, VT 05841

802-533-2647

EMAIL
highland.lodge@
verizon.net

URL
www.highlandlodge.
com/

HIGHLAND LODGE
Vermont Cheddar and Beer Cheese

1 pound Vermont sharp
   cheddar cheese
1 clove garlic, mashed
1½ tablespoons Worcestershire
   sauce

½ teaspoon dry mustard
¼ bottle of beer
Tabasco to taste

Cube the cheddar, then process until smooth. Add the garlic, Worcestershire, mustard, and Tabasco.

   Add the beer a little at a time, with the machine still running until it is a good spreading consistency. Serve with crackers.

T H E   B E R N E R H O F   I N N

Spaetzle - German Egg Dumplings

THE BERNERHOF INN

PO Box 240
Glen, NH 03838

603-383-9132

EMAIL
stay@bernerhofinn.com
URL
www.bernerhofinn.com

For the spaetzle:
2¾ cups flour
1 cup milk
3 to 4 eggs, beaten
A scant teaspoon of salt, fresh
    white pepper, freshly grated
    nutmeg

For cooking and serving the
spaetzle:
2 quarts rapidly boiling,
    lightly salted & oiled water
    (approx. 1 tablespoon oil)
4 tablespoons butter
4 tablespoons fresh chopped
    parsley

Combine the flour, milk, and spices in a bowl and, mixing with a whisk, add enough eggs to obtain a thick but fairly loose paste. Let stand for 5 minutes.

Using a spaetzle cutter, or an improvisation thereof, cut small bits of dough into the boiling water which has the salt and oil. (This prevents the dumplings from sticking together.)

The spaetzle can be prepared up to 48 hours ahead of time to this stage and stored in cold water.

To serve the spaetzle, drain thoroughly. Sauté them in foaming butter in a large frying pan, sprinkling with parsley, salt and pepper.

Alternative: Freshly cooked spaetzle can be served with melted butter or sour cream.

Yield: 7 servings

Entrées

For centuries, roadway inns have provided weary travelers with a warm and very welcomed meal. Today, many country inns and lodges pride themselves on their fine cuisine and have even become destinations for fine dining. I'll never forget the night I checked into a quaint country inn and restaurant in rural Pennsylvania at ten o'clock at night to find the dining room packed. The hosts were galling guests with wine, cheeses, custom made liquors, and an absolutely outrageous chocolate mousse. The place was packed! The comaraderie was evident. What better way to end a long day of travel than in the company of those who appreciate the finer things in life. Most of the retinue retired sometime later to waiting guestrooms upstairs. Another thing that really impresses me with country inn cuisine is that much of it has evolved with a sense of place over many years and combines the best of local ingredients with the flair that comes from exposure to many ethnic influences.

We've chosen the recipes in this chapter because they're all so special and are in every instance the "most requested."

10TH AVENUE INN B&B
Sumptuous Salmon Crumpets

10TH AVENUE INN
B&B

125 10th Avenue
Seaside, OR 97138

503-738-0643

EMAIL
stay@10aveinn.com

URL
www.10aveinn.com

1 package best quality muffins
1 16-ounce can Alaskan Pink Salmon, drained and cleaned
1 pound Mozarella cheese, grated
1 small bunch of fresh chives, chopped

2 tablespoons mayonnaise
Sprinkle McIlhenny tabasco sauce
Salt & pepper
Muenster cheese slices
Strips of smoked lox
Parsley

Each serving will require one toasted English muffin sliced in two. Clean and drain one 16-oz. can of Alaskan Pink Salmon. Break the salmon up with a fork into a bowl.

Chop a small bunch of chives to sprinkle into the salmon. Grate one pound of Mozarella cheese and add to the mixture. Add just enough mayonaise to bind. Sprinkle salt and pepper on top with plenty of McIlhenny Tobasco sauce.

Spread even amounts of the mixture onto each English muffin and slice Muenster cheese slices into ¼ inch strips. Make a criss-cross on top of the topped muffins and add just a bit of smoked lox and some parsley flakes for color. Broil until golden brown. Serve hot.

Yield: 3 servings

Cooking Time: 30 min.

GREYHOUSE INN

1115 Hwy 93 S
Salmon, ID 83467

208-756-3968

EMAIL
osgood@hughes.net

URL
www.greyhouseinn.
com

G R E Y H O U S E   I N N
Barbecue Chicken Sandwiches

2 tablespoons rice vinegar
1 tablespoon mayonnaise
1 tablespoon sugar
¼ teaspoon Tabasco sauce
¼ teaspoon salt
2 cups shredded cole slaw mix
½ cup shredded carrots

½ cup thinly sliced red onion
2 tablespoons cilantro leaves
4 skinless, boneless chicken
   breast halves 1¼ lb.
½ cup spicy barbecue sauce,
   divided
4 hamburger buns

In a medium bowl, combine rice vinegar, mayonnaise, sugar, tabasco and salt. Toss in coleslaw, carrots, sliced red onion, and cilantro leaves. Set aside.

Gently pound chicken to flatten slightly. Spread top of each breast half with 1 teaspoon BBQ sauce, and broil 3–4 minutes or until cooked through.

Tear chicken into shreds with 2 forks by skewering with one and pulling the other. Heat shredded chicken with remaining barbecue sauce. Serve chicken on buns, topped with remaining barbecue sauce and coleslaw.

Yield: 4 servings

CHESTNUT STREET INN

Seared Scallop with Avocado and North African Mango Chutney

2 lbs. mango, peeled & chopped
2 Tbsp extra virgin olive oil
½ tsp Harissa
½ red onion, diced
½ red bell pepper, seeded & diced
2 cloves garlic, minced
pinch ground ginger
pinch Saffron
pinch Kosher salt & pepper
4 oz orange juice
2 oz red wine vinegar
½ cup honey
½ tsp orange zest
1 tsp orange blossom water
2 tsps ras el hanout
pinch Kosher salt & pepper
¼ cup dried cranberries
¼ cup toasted pistachios
4 scallops
pinch Kosher salt & pepper
pinch Hungarian hot paprika
2 tsps unsalted butter
¼ cup dry sherry
1 avocado

CHESTNUT STREET INN

PO Box 25
Sheffield, IL 61361

815-454-2419

EMAIL
monikaandjeff@
chestnut-inn.com

URL
www.chestnut-inn.com

Heat olive oil in a med. sauté pan over med. high heat. Add onion, sauté until translucent, approx. 5 mins. Add harissa and heat through 1 min. Add garlic and sauté until fragrant. Add bell pepper, ginger, saffron, salt & pepper and sauté an additional minute until the spices are toasted. Add mango and sauté 1 minute to heat through. Turn off. Add OJ, vinegar, honey, orange zest, orange blossom water and ras el hanout to the pan. Turn back on and bring to a boil. Reduce heat to a simmer, cook approx. 30 mins or until the liquid has mostly evaporated and the chutney has thickened. Season to taste. Transfer to a bowl over an ice bath. Add cranberries & pistachios and stir to combine. Once cooled, cover with plastic wrap and place in the refrigerator. Let sit at least 4 hours or up to overnight for the flavors to mature.

Pat scallops dry with a paper towel. Season with salt, pepper and paprika on one side. Heat butter in a med. sauté pan over med. high heat until the butter begins to brown. Add scallops & sear on one side. Turn over and deglaze the pan with sherry. Continue cooking until the scallops are cooked through but not rubbery, approx. 5 mins. To serve, place a Tbsp of chutney on a small plate. Cut the avocado into quarters and place one quarter over the chutney. Top with seared scallop and serve immediately.

Yield: 4 servings   Cooking Time: 45 min.

THE STONEBOW INN

146 Casselman Rd
Grantsville, MD 21536

301-895-4250

EMAIL
info@stonebowinn.com

URL
www.stonebowinn.com

THE STONEBOW INN

Goat Cheese and Spinach Frittata

3 Tbsp extra-virgin olive oil
8 thin slices of pancetta
1 small leek, sliced and chopped fine
1½ cups baby spinach
12 large eggs, beaten
5 ounces Firefly Farms Allegheny Chevre goat cheese, crumbled
Your favorite hot sauce
Salt and pepper to taste

Preheat the oven to 400°F. Heat the olive oil in a medium skillet and cook the pancetta until crisp. Transfer to paper towels on a plate to cool, then crumble it and set aside.

Add the leek to the skillet and cook until softened about 3 minutes. Add the spinach and cook until wilted, about 3 more minutes. Transfer the mix to a small bowl and set aside.

For each fritatta:

Whisk 3 eggs in a small bowl with a splash of hot sauce, salt, pepper and a tablespoon of water. Wrap the handle of an 8–9 inch skillet in foil and heat over moderate heat; spray with canola oil and melt 1 tablespoon of butter until the foam subsides. Pour in the eggs and cook, stirring, until curds begin to form. Scatter ¼ of the pancetta, leek and spinach mix and crumbled goat cheese over the eggs and stir them in slightly. Transfer the skillet to the oven and bake until the eggs are set, about 5 minutes.

Remove the skillet from the oven and brown the top of the fittata with a chef's blowtorch until bubbly and brown in spots. Slide the frittata onto a cutting board, slice in half and serve with oven-roasted tomatoes and toast.

Yield: 4 servings

Cooking Time: 10 min.

NAGLE WARREN MANSION

Grilled Beef Tenderloin with Red Wine & Pistachios

NAGLE WARREN
MANSION

222 E 17th St
Cheyenne, WY 82001

307-637-3333

EMAIL
jim@nwmbb.com

URL
www.
naglewarrenmansion.
com

For the red wine sauce:
6 cups beef or veal stock
6 cups dry red wine, preferably Pinot Noir
1½ cups garlic cloves, roasted
1½ cups shallots, chopped
1½ cups fresh parsley, chopped
Salt to taste
Fresh ground pepper to taste

For the grilled beef:
¾ cup toasted pistachios, chopped
¾ cup sunflower seeds, chopped
6 lbs. beef tenderloin, cut into 12, 8-oz steaks
6 tablespoons olive or corn oil
12 sprigs fresh parsley, for garnish

Preheat the grill and preheat oven to 300°F

In a large saucepan, combine the stock, red wine, ½ cup of the roasted garlic, the shallots and ¾ cup of the chopped parsley. Bring to a simmer over medium heat and cook until reduced to coat the back of a spoon, about 20 minutes.

Transfer mixture to a blender and puree until smooth. Strain through a fine sieve into another clean saucepan, then adjust the salt and pepper. Stir in the remaining parsley, then reduce heat to low.

In a small bowl, combine the remaining garlic, the pistachios, sunflower seeds and 6 tablespoons of the Red Wine sauce. Mix well and set aside. Rub the surface of the steaks with the olive or corn oil.

Grill the steaks until well seared on the surface—both sides. Place in a baking dish. Bake at 300°F for about 5–7 minutes for medium-rare, depending on the thickness.

Brush the tops of the steaks with a small amount of Red Wine sauce, and then press the steaks, topside down, into the pistachio mixture, coating the surface well. Position the steaks on serving platter, spoon the remaining sauce around them, garnish with parsley sprigs and serve.

Yield: 6

AFTON HOUSE INN

PO Box 326
Afton, MN 55001

651-436-8883

EMAIL
kathy@aftonhouseinn.
com

URL
www.aftonhouseinn.
com

AFTON HOUSE INN

Espresso Crusted Beef Strip with Vegetable Accompaniments

Steak:
2 10-ounce New York strip
    steaks
½ ounce espresso, ground
1 ounce black truffles, shaved,
    or ½ ounce truffle oil
salt and pepper

Purée:
6 parsnips, cleaned and peeled
1 tablespoon cumin
1 bay leaf
3 cups vegetable stock

Swiss Chard:
2 heads swiss chard, julienned
¼ shallot, sliced
¼ ounce garlic, chopped
1 ounce white wine
½ ounce cold butter

Honey Thyme Glaze:
2 ounces fresh demi-glace
2 sprigs thyme, cleaned
¼ ounce clover honey

Steak: Dust beef with espresso, salt, and pepper. Pan-sear on medium-high heat and finish in a 350° oven for 10–15 minutes (for medium).

Purée: Chop parsnips and sauté with cumin, shallots, bay leaf, and garlic. Deglaze with vegetable stock, simmer for 10 minutes, and purée with a hand mixer. Season and finish with butter.

Glaze: Mix demi-glace, thyme, and honey. Warm to a simmer.

Swiss chard: Sauté swiss chard with shallots and garlic and season with salt and pepper. Deglaze with white wine and finish with butter.

Yield: 2 servings

Cooking Time: 30 min.

ABINGDON MANOR INN &
RESTAURANT

Parsleyed Rack of Lamb

ABINGDON MANOR
INN & RESTAURANT

307 Church St
Latta, SC 29565

843-752-5090

EMAIL
abingdon@bellsouth.net

URL
www.abingdonmanor.
com

2 racks of lamb, about 2½
  pounds, Frenched
salt and freshly ground pepper
  to taste
4 tbsp butter
½ cup bread crumbs
3 tbsp chopped parsley
1 clove garlic, finely minced
1 shallot, finely minced
1 tsp olive oil

Shallot-Balsamic Reduction
2 tsp olive or vegetable oil
1 tbsp unsalted butter
1 tbsp finely chopped shallot
¼ cup homemade beef broth, or
  low-sodium canned broth
2 tbsp Balsamic vinegar

Heat skillet and add butter and shallot. Cook stirring almost constantly, until the shallot softens, approximately 1 minute.

Add the broth and increase the heat to high. Boil, scraping up the browned bits in the skillet with a wooden spoon, until the broth is reduced to 2 tablespoons, approximately 1 minute.

Stir in the vinegar and cook for 30 seconds.

Preheat broiler to high. If the oven is heated separately, preheat it also to 500°.

Rub with butter a baking dish large enough to hold the racks of lamb in one layer and close together. Place the racks, meat side down, in the dish and dot the ribs with 2 tablespoons of butter.

Meanwhile, combine the bread crumbs, parsley, garlic, shallot, and olive oil in a bowl.

Place the racks of lamb under the broiler and cook about 2 or 3 minutes. Turn and cook about 2 or 3 minutes.

Sprinkle the meaty side of the ribs with the bread crumbs mixture. Melt the remaining 2 tablespoons of butter and pour over the ribs. Place in the oven and bake 8–10 minutes, depending on the degree of doneness desired.

Allow to cool slightly and carve into chops. Serve with Shallot-Balsamic Vinegar Sauce.

Yield: 4 servings

Cooking Time: 30 min.

OLDE CAPTAIN'S INN

101 Main St, Rt 6A
Yarmouth Port, MA
02675

508-362-4496

EMAIL
general@
oldecaptainsinn.com

URL
www.oldecaptainsinn.
com

OLDE CAPTAIN'S INN
Swedish Meatballs

¾ lb lean ground beef
¼ lb ground pork
½ lb ground veal
1½ cups soft breadcrumbs
½ cup chopped onion
1 egg
1¼ tsp salt
1 cup light cream
1 Tbsp butter or margarine plus
2 Tbsp butter or margarine
¼ cup finely snipped parsley
Dash pepper
Dash ground nutmeg
Dash ground ginger

Have meats ground together twice. Soak bread in cream about 5 minutes. Cook onion in tablespoon butter until tender, but not brown. Mix meats, crumb mixture, onion, egg, parsley, and seasonings. Beat 5 minutes at medium speed in mixer or mix by hand until well combined. Shape into 1½ inch balls. (Mixture will be soft, for easier shaping, wet hands and chill mixture first.)

Brown meatballs in 2 tablespoons butter in skillet. Remove from pan, keep warm. Stir in 2 tablespoons flour. Add 1 beef bouillon cube dissolved in 1¼ cups boiling water and ½ teaspoon instant coffee powder. Cook and stir until gravy thickens. Add meatballs. Cover and cook slowly, about 30 minutes. Baste occasionally. Serve warm.

Yield: 2 dozen

INN & SPA AT CEDAR FALLS

Pork Roast with Peppercorn-Mustard Crust and Cider Gravy

INN & SPA AT CEDAR
FALLS

21190 State Rt 374
Logan, OH 43138

740-385-7489

EMAIL
info@innatcedarfalls.
com

URL
www.innatcedarfalls.
com

¼ cup plus 1 tablespoon butter,
   room temperature
1 tablespoon cracked white
   peppercorn
1 4½ lb boneless pork loin roast
   rolled and tied
1 tablespoon whole mustard
   seeds
2 tablespoons all purpose flour
2 teaspoon golden brown sugar
2 tablespoons Dijon mustard
2 teaspoon dried thyme,
   crumbled

1 tablespoon cracked black
   peppercorns
1 tablespoon cracked dried
   green peppercorns

For the Cider Gravy:
1½ cups apple cider
3 tablespoons apple jack
1 tablespoon all purpose flour
¾ cup chicken broth
1 tablespoon cider vinegar
1 teaspoon Dijon mustard
Salt and pepper

Pork Roast: Position rack in lowest third of oven and preheat to 475 degrees. Add 1 tablespoon butter to a heavy large skillet over medium-high heat and brown about 4 minutes per side. Remove from skillet. Cool 10 minutes. Transfer to roasting pan.

Combine remaining ¼ cup butter with mustard seeds, flour, sugar, mustard, thyme, and peppercorns in bowl. Spread paste oven top and sides of roast. Roast 30 min. Reduce heat to 325°.

Continue cooking until internal temperature reads 160°F about 1 hour 20 minutes. Transfer roast to cutting board and tent with foil. Transfer 2 tablespoons drippings in pan to heavy small saucepan; discard remaining drippings.

Cider Gravy: Heat roasting pan over medium-low heat. Add cider and boil until liquid is reduced to ¾ cup scraping up any browned bits, about 8 minutes. Stir in apple jack, boil 1 minute.

Heat drippings in saucepan over medium-high heat. Add flour and stir until golden brown, about 2 minutes. Whisk in cider mixture and stock. Simmer until thickened, stirring occasionally, about 2 minutes. Remove from heat. Mix in vinegar and mustard. Season with salt and pepper. Carve roast and serve with gravy.

Yield: 8

CLIFF COTTAGE INN
LUXURY B&BEUREKA
SPRINGS, AR 72632

479-253-7409

EMAIL
cliffcottage@sbcglobal.
net

URL
www.cliffcottage.com/

CLIFF COTTAGE INN LUXURY B & B

Golden Apricot-Glazed Porkchops

6 pork loin chops, 1 inch thick
¼ cup all-purpose flour for
    dredging pork
2 tablespoons peanut oil
½ cup Sautérnes or other sweet
    white wine
¼ cup Meyers dark rum
⅓ cup apricot jam
1 teaspoon Pick-a-peppa sauce
1 tablespoon freshly-squeezed
    lime juice

2 teaspoons curry powder
Several dashes of Tabasco sauce
1 tablespoon cilantro, freshly
    minced
6 fresh apricots
1½ bunches greens (parsley,
    cilantro or kale)
Fruit chutney for garnishing
Coconut shredded and
    unsweetened for garnish

Preheat oven to 375 degrees.

Trim excess fat off chops and dredge with flour. Heat oil over medium-high heat and brown chops in oil.

Place browned chops in 9 inch square baking pan.

Combine wine, rum, jam, Pick-a-peppa, lime juice, curry and Tabasco in a small bowl and pour over chops.

Cover tightly with foil and bake in 375 degree oven for 1 hour.

Before serving, sprinkle cilantro over top of pork chops. Halve and pit the apricots and place on greens. Fill center of apricots with spoonful of any fruit chutney and sprinkle chutney with shredded coconut. Place pork chops next to garnish and serve.

Yield: 6 servings

DEVILS TOWER LODGE

Trapper's Peak Tenderloin

DEVILS TOWER
LODGE

PO Box 66
Devils Tower, WY 82714

307-467-5267

EMAIL
frank@
devilstowerlodge.com

URL
www.devilstowerlodge.
com

4 pounds whole beef tenderloin
2 to 4 cloves garlic, minced
4 to 6 tablespoons coarsely
    ground black pepper
¾ cup Worchestershire sauce
1½ cups soy Sauce
1⅓ cups undiluted beef bouillon

Mushroom-Roquefort Sauce:
¼ pound roquefort cheese
½ cup butter
2 to 4 cloves garlic, minced
1 tablespoon Worchestershire
    sauce
¼ teaspoon caraway seeds
½ cup of chopped green onions,
    including tops
½ pound mushrooms, sliced

Wash tenderloin and pat dry. Rub with minced garlic and press black pepper onto sides. Combine Worchestershire sauce and soy sauce in large dish and marinate for 2–3 hours at room temperature.

Preheat oven to 500 degrees. Drain and discard marinade. Pour bouillon around beef. Put into oven and immediately reduce heat to 350 degrees.

Cook for 18 minutes per pound for rare, 20 minutes per pound for medium rare, or until internal temperature reaches 135–140 degrees.

Prepare sauce: In medium saucepan, over low heat, combine cheese, butter, garlic, Worchestershire sauce and caraway seeds. Stir until cheese and butter melt. Add green onions and mushrooms. Continue cooking for 2–3 minutes.

Slice meat and serve with Mushroom-Roquefort Sauce.

An impressive, yet conservatively elegant presentation for family or guests.

Yield: 6 or more servings

EAGLES MERE INN

PO Box 356
Eagles Mere, PA 17731

570-525-3273

EMAIL
relax@eaglesmereinn.
com

URL
www.eaglesmereinn.
com

EAGLES MERE INN
West Indian Rum Stew

4 cups onion, chopped
1 bay leaf
2 lbs. roasted meat cubes of
    your choice, ¾ inch
2 teaspoons fresh garlic, pressed
1 teaspoon freshly ground black
    pepper
1 tablespoon sugar
1 green pepper, cut into
    julienne ¼ inch × 2 inch
1 red pepper, cut into julienne
    ¼ inch × 2 inch

1 yellow pepper, cut into
    julienne ¼ inch × 2 inch
2 fresh tomatoes, chopped
1 cup water
⅓ cup tomato paste
1 teaspoon Tabasco sauce
1 teaspoon Vietnamese fish
    sauce
⅓ cup pimiento stuffed green
    olives
¼ cup Meyer's Dark Rum

Preheat oven to 325°F.

Layer first ten ingredients in a 9×13 in casserole dish.

Combine, water, tomato paste, Tabasco, and fish sauce in a small bowl and pour mixture on ingredients in pan, cover and bake in 325° oven for 45 minutes.

Just before serving or storing, add and mix in olives and rum.

1 2 9 1   B E D   &   B R E A K F A S T

Sliced Veal in a Creamy Mushroom Sauce

1 lb thinly sliced, lean veal
  shoulder
1 diced medium-white onion
2 cups sliced mushrooms
1 Tbsp ground black pepper
1 cup brown gravy

½ cup heavy whipping cream
2 Tbsp olive oil
1 cup white wine
1 tsp paprika powder or 1 tsp
  finely chopped parsley for
  garnish

In a large skillet, sauté thinly sliced veal in olive oil for two minutes. Add sliced mushrooms and onions and stir for 30 seconds.

Remove mixture and place in bowl. Sauté white wine and gravy in same skillet for five minutes. Return veal, onions and mushrooms to skillet, add cream and cook 1 minute. Add pepper and serve immediately.

Garnish with parsley and paprika powder.

1291 BED &
BREAKFAST

337 W 55th St
New York City, NY
10019

212-397-9686

EMAIL
1291@1291.com

URL
www.1291.com

GREYHOUSE INN

1115 Hwy 93 S
Salmon, ID 83467

208-756-3968

EMAIL
osgood@hughes.net

URL
www.greyhouseinn.
com

GREYHOUSE INN

Bison Tenderloin Steaks with Mushrooms

Mushrooms:

½ lb. fresh mushrooms, whole
 if very small, quartered if
 large
2 Tbsp butter
1 Tbsp oil

2 Tbsp minced shallots or green
 onions
¼ tsp salt
Pinch of pepper

Sauté mushrooms in hot butter and oil for 5 minutes to brown them lightly, stir in shallots/onions and cook slowly for a minute or two more. Season and set aside.

Steaks:

6 bison fillet steaks, 1 inch thick
 and 2½ inch in diameter,
 each wrapped in a strip of
 bacon
2 Tbsp butter, more if needed

1 Tbsp oil
1 or 2 heavy skillets just large
 enough to hold the steaks
 easily

Dry the steaks on paper towels. Place the butter and oil in the skillet and set over moderately high heat. When you see the butter foam begin to subside, indicating it is hot enough to sear and brown the bison steaks, sauté them for 3–4 minutes on each side.

They are medium rare if, when pressed with your finger, they offer a suggestion of resistance in contrast to their soft, raw state. Bison should be eaten medium or rare.

Salt and pepper and serve on a warm platter. Discard a strip of fat if you wish.

A handsome presentation for these steaks is a platter decorated with whole baked tomatoes, artichoke hearts cooked in butter.

Serve with them a good red Bordeaux.

MILLBROOK INN & RESTAURANT
Three Cheese Fettuccine

MILLBROOK INN &
RESTAURANT

533 Mill Brook Rd
Waitsfield, VT 05673

802-496-2405

EMAIL
gorman@millbrookinn.
com

URL
www.millbrookinn.com

2 tablespoons scallions, chopped
3 tablespoons sun-dried
   tomatoes, chopped
1 tablespoons olive oil
1 cup white wine
½ lb extra sharp cheddar cheese,
   grated
½ cup mascarpone cheese
¼ cup fresh grated parmesan
   cheese
1 lb homemade or fresh
   fettuccine noodles

In a frying pan, sauté scallions and sun-dried tomatoes in olive oil until soft. Add white wine and cheddar. Cook over medium heat until the cheese melts. Add the mascarpone cheese, stirring until blended.

Cook noodles to package directions. Toss with the sauce until coated. Divide among 4 dinner plates and top with grated parmesan.

COBBLE HOUSE INN

PO Box 49
Gaysville, VT 05746

802-234-5458

EMAIL
unwind@
cobblehouseinn.com

URL
www.cobblehouseinn.
com

C O B B L E   H O U S E   I N N

Rigatoni with Zucchini and Prosciutto

½ teaspoon salt
¾ lb. rigatoni pasta
1 cup chicken broth
3 (6 oz.) zucchini or yellow
    squash or combination
    sliced into 1½ inch sticks
1¼ cups low fat milk

2 tablespoons flour
½ teaspoon ground black pepper
¼ cup Parmesan cheese
6 thin slices prosciutto chopped
3 tablespoons chives
1 tablespoon unsalted butter

In a large pot, bring 4 quarts water and 1 teaspoon salt to a boil. Add pasta: cook according to package directions. Drain and place into large pasta bowl.

In a large skillet heat ½ cup broth until simmering. Add squash and cook over high heat 3 to 5 minutes, until crisp-tender. Remove, place squash in a bowl and cover.

In small bowl, whisk remaining broth, milk, flour, remaining salt and pepper until smooth and pour into skillet. Bring to a boil, reduce heat to a simmer, stirring 1 minute, until slightly thickened. Remove from heat. Stir in parmesan, prosciutto, chives and butter.

Pour sauce over pasta, add squash, toss and serve.

Yield: 4

THE COMBES FAMILY INN

Macaroni and Cheese

THE COMBES FAMILY INN

953 E Lake Rd
Ludlow, VT 05149
802-228-8799
EMAIL
billcfi@tds.net
URL
www.combesfamilyinn.com/

7 ounces of dry macaroni (1¾ cups—about 2 ounces of dry per ½ cup)
3 tablespoons butter
3 tablespoons flour
¼ teaspoon salt

dash pepper
2 cups milk
2 cups shredded American or cheddar cheese
¼ cup bread crumbs
1 tablespoon melted butter

Preheat oven to 350°F.

Cook macaroni, following package directions. Drain and rinse. Melt butter in saucepan, blend in flour, salt, and pepper. Add milk. Cook, stirring constantly until mixture thickens. Stir in 1 cup of cheese until melted.

Combine cheese mixture and macaroni. Fold in remaining cheese. Pour in greased 2 quart casserole. Combine bread crumbs and melted butter. Sprinkle on top of casserole. Bake in 350°F oven for 30 to 40 minutes until lightly brown and bubbly.

Yield: 6 servings

GENESEE COUNTRY
INN B&B

PO Box 226
Mumford, NY 14511

585-538-2500

EMAIL
stay@
geneseecountryinn.com

URL
www.
geneseecountryinn.com

GENESEE COUNTRY INN B&B

Pasta Frittata

3 to 4 eggs
2 plum tomatoes, chopped
4 ounces bite sized cooked pasta
1 (14 once) can artichokes in water, drained and sliced
4–6 ounces cubed mozzarella cheese
3–4 tablespoons grated Parmesan cheese
3 to 4 tablespoons chopped parsley
2 tablespoons olive oil for frying

Combine all ingredients, except oil. Pour oil, and then Frittata ingredients, into a heated nonstick frying pan. Cook over medium low flame until set. Flip over and continue to cook until omelet is solid. Serve in wedges.

Yield: 2

THE MANGO INN
Mango-Mustard Glazed Chicken

THE MANGO INN

128 N Lakeside Dr
Lake Worth, FL 33460

561-533-6900

EMAIL
info@mangoinn.com

URL
www.mangoinn.com

1 cup chopped peeled mango
1 cup pineapple juice
½ cup apricot or peach
    preserves
½ cup dry white wine
1 ½ tablespoons stone-ground
    mustard

1 tablespoon cornstarch
1 tablespoon water
6 (4-ounce) skinned, boned
    chicken breast halves
¼ teaspoon salt
¼ teaspoon pepper
Cooking spray

Combine first 7 ingredients in a bowl; stir well with a whisk.

Sprinkle chicken with salt and pepper. Heat a large non-stick skillet coated with cooking spray over medium heat until hot. Add chicken; cook 3 minutes on each side or until browned. Remove chicken from pan.

Add mango mixture; bring to a boil. Return chicken to pan; reduce heat, and simmer 15 minutes or until chicken is done and sauce thickens, stirring occasionally.

Yield: 6 servings

GRANDISON INN AT
MANEY PARK

1200 N Shartel Ave
Oklahoma City, OK
73103

405-232-8778

EMAIL
grandison@coxinet.net

URL
www.grandisoninn.
com

GRANDISON INN
AT MANEY PARK

Cornish Hens Baked in Champagne

2 Cornish hens
Salt
¼ cup melted butter
Freshly ground pepper

¼ cup champagne
Cooked rice or pasta of your
choice

Clean the hens and remove the organs. Lightly salt the cavities.
Brush with melted butter and lay in a baking pan, breast side up.
Pepper the hens to taste. Bake in a 425 degree oven for 10 minutes
to brown. Reduce the heat to 350 degrees, pour champagne over
the hens and return to the oven for 30 to 45 minutes. Baste every
5 minutes (this seems like a lot, but it is well worth the flavor
result).

Serve the hens whole or split over the bed of rice or pasta.
Serves 2, or 4 if split. Also excellent served with a side of buttered
brussel sprouts.

Yield: 4 servings

ST. CHARLES GUEST HOUSE

Chicken Jambalaya

1 large chicken fryer, cut up
2 quarts water
2 teaspoons salt
3 cups uncooked 'converted' rice
2 bay leaves
2 pounds smoked sausage
1 large white onion, chopped
1 large green pepper, chopped
2 cloves garlic, minced

1 cup coarsely chopped celery
½ teaspoon hot sauce (optional)
2 bay leaves
¼ teaspoon cayenne or red pepper (optional)
1 15-ounce can tomato sauce
1 10-ounce can chopped tomatoes
½ cup chopped green onions

Boil the chicken pieces in a large pot with water and salt. When tender, remove the chicken, reserving the stock. Tear the meat, discarding the skin, into bite-sized pieces.

Cook the rice in 7 cups of the reserved stock seasoned with 2 bay leaves.

While the rice cooks, cut the sausage into bite-sized pieces and sauté with the onion, green pepper, garlic, celery, hot sauce, 2 bay leaves and cayenne pepper. Cook until tender, skim off the fat and add the tomato sauce and tomatoes. Combine with the rice and the chicken pieces. Let the mixture sit for a while for flavors to mingle. When ready to serve, add raw chopped green onions.

Serve with hot crispy bread and a good green salad with vinaigrette dressing.

ST. CHARLES GUEST HOUSE

1748 Prytania St
New Orleans, LA 70130

504-523-6556

EMAIL
dhilton111@aol.com

URL
www.
stcharlesguesthouse.
com

INN & SPA AT CEDAR FALLS

21190 State Rt 374
Logan, OH 43138

740-385-7489

EMAIL
info@innatcedarfalls.com

URL
www.innatcedarfalls.com

INN & SPA AT CEDAR FALLS

Lemon Chicken

*8 skinless, boneless chicken
   breasts*
*1 cup fresh lemon juice, about 8
   lemons*
1 cup flour
1 teaspoon paprika

*½ teaspoon freshly ground
   black pepper*
¼ cup oil
1 tablespoon grated lemon zest
2 tablespoons brown sugar
2 tablespoons chicken stock
2 lemons, sliced paper thin

Preheat oven to 350°F.

Combine chicken and lemon juice in a bowl just large enough to hold them comfortably. Cover and marinate in refrigerator for 30 minutes, turning once.

Drain chicken thoroughly and pat dry. Fill a plastic bag with flour, paprika and black pepper and shake to mix. Put two pieces of chicken into the bag and shake coating completely.

Heat oil in frying pan until hot. Fry chicken pieces a few at a time, do not crowd pan, until brown and crisp. This will take about 6–8 minutes per batch.

Arrange chicken in a single layer in a shallow baking pan. Sprinkle evenly with lemon zest and brown sugar. Mix chicken stock and lemon juice together and pour around chicken pieces. Put a slice of lemon on top of each piece of chicken. Bake chicken for 35 to 40 minutes, until golden brown.

Yield: 8 servings

SMUGGLER'S NOTCH INN
The Chef's Drunken Chicken

SMUGGLER'S NOTCH
INN

PO Box 129
Jeffersonville, VT 05464

802-644-6607

EMAIL
info@smuggsinn.com

URL
www.smuggsinn.com

1 8-oz boneless, skinless
   chicken breast
¼ of an apple, sinned and sliced
1 oz mild cheddar cheese
flour to coat chicken

1 egg beaten
¼ cup bread crumbs
oil for sautéing
¼ cup cream sherry

Preheat oven to 375°F.

Butterfly each chicken breast by splitting each breast in half, without cutting all the way through and pound to about ¼ inch in thickness.

Place apple and cheese inside breast and close with toothpicks. Roll the breast in flour.

Then dip the chicken in the beaten egg and roll it in the bread crumbs until it is completely covered. Sauté in the oil until golden brown all over. Let cool and remove toothpicks.

When ready to make, place in small baking dish and pour sherry over the top. Bake 15 minutes at 375°F.

Enjoy!

Yield: 1 servings

1870 BANANA
COURTYARD

New Orleans, LA 70116
504-947-4475
EMAIL
bananacour@aol.com
URL
www.bananacourtyard.
com

1 8 7 0   B A N A N A   C O U R T Y A R D

Crawfish or Shrimp Maquechoux

⅓ cup bacon drippings or olive oil

2 packages** frozen crawfish tails, thawed. Or, 1 package crawfish and 1 pound fresh medium shrimp, peeled and deveined. Substitute: If crawfish not available, use all shrimp. (**Note: crawfish tails are fairly widely available now, in the frozen seafood section, usually in 12 or 16 ounce packages. They are already parboiled, so don't overcook).

6 cups of fresh white corn, cut off cob. If white corn is not available substitute yellow corn, but it's not as traditional. Substitute 1 pound frozen corn if fresh is not available

2 tablespoons heavy cream

3 cups chopped onion

1 cup bell pepper, chopped

3 large creole tomatoes, coarsely chopped. If good, flavorful fresh tomatoes aren't available, substitute one can chopped tomatoes, using only half the liquid.

2 tablespoons finely chopped fresh flat, Italian parsley. If ingredient not available, omit.

2 tablespoons salt

Juice of ½ lemon

1 teaspoon, or more to taste, freshly ground black pepper OR Banana Courtyard Famous 3-Pep Seasoning.

½ cup dry white wine

½ stick butter

½ teaspoon Tabasco or other hot sauce

Marinate crawfish in the white wine and the juice of ½ lemon. When you cut the kernels off the cob, then scrape the cob, with a knife, to get the liquid. Add the cob liquid. If fresh corn isn't in season, substitute can or frozen corn and add 3 extra tablespoons heavy cream in place of corn cob liquid.

In a large iron skillet, heat the oil over medium heat. Sauté the bell peppers, about 3 minutes, then add onions—cover skillet to speed process. When bell pepper and onion are softened, lower the heat—try not to brown them. Remove and reserve this in a bowl. Put the corn, corn liquid, butter, and cream, in the skillet. Mix thoroughly. Cook on medium heat, 10 minutes. Add tomatoes, reserved onion and bell pepper, plus salt and pepper and cook over medium heat for 5 minutes, stirring frequently.

Add crawfish and shrimp, part of the marinade, white wine, then cook for 4–6 minutes, stirring frequently.

If mixture seems too dry, add 2–3 tablespoons of reserved marinade or chicken stock, toward end of cooking period. Taste for seasoning.

Serve hot in wide soup bowls. This dish is even better when refrigerated for several hours or overnight and reheated before serving. If you are already an experienced Cajun cook, please excuse the level of detail in this recipe.

'Maquechoux', pronounced mock shoe, is a Cajun word for a smothered dish made with fresh corn.

Yield: 5 servings

SELAH INN ON HOOD
CANAL

210 NE Cherokee Beach
Belfair, WA 98528

360-275-0916

EMAIL
innkeeper@selahinn.
com

URL
www.selahinn.com

SELAH INN ON HOOD CANAL

Garlic Roasted Dungeness Crab

4 dungeness crabs, cleaned,
   cooked & cracked
⅓ cup butter
⅓ cup olive oil
3 tablespoons minced garlic

Salt & pepper to taste
3 tablespoons freshly squeezed
   lemon juice
¼ cup chopped fresh parsley

Preheat the oven to 500°F. Heat butter, oil, and garlic is a large saucepan over medium-high heat. Add crabs, 2 at a time, toss well, season with salt & pepper.

Transfer to a large baking pan. Roast about 12 minutes, tossing well halfway through. Warm butter mixture, add lemon juice and parsley.

Arrange crabs in a large shallow bowl and drizzle butter mixture over. Serve immediately with chunks of hot bread and a nice white wine.

GOLDEN PHEASANT INN

Grilled Swordfish with Cilantro-Lime Butter

½ cup butter, softened
⅓ cup cilantro, freshly chopped
½ tablespoon jalapeno chile
   pepper, chopped
1 tablespoon lime zest, finely
   chopped

1 tablespoon lime juice
8 6-ounce swordfish steaks (1
   inch thick)
¼ cup olive oil

GOLDEN PHEASANT
INN

763 River Rd
Erwinna, PA 18920

610-294-9595

EMAIL
barbara@
goldenpheasant.com

URL
www.goldenpheasant.
com

Combine butter, cilantro, jalepeno pepper, lime zest and lime juice in a small non reactive bowl.

Brush fish steaks with olive oil on both sides. Grill on an oiled grill rack or in a fish grilling basket over medium hot coals. Grill 4–6 minutes, or until fish begins to flake easily when tested with a fork. Turn once, and finish grilling approximately 4–6 minutes more.

Serve with dab of butter mixture on each steak.

Yield: 8 servings

Cooking Time: 30 min.

PROSPECT HILL
PLANTATION INN &
RESTAURANT

Charlottesville, VA
22906

540-967-0844

EMAIL
info@prospecthill.com
URL
www.prospecthill.com

PROSPECT HILL PLANTATION INN & RESTAURANT

Chesapeake Bay Crab Mousse Roulade

1 pound fresh crab meat, picked over to remove any shell bits
2 eggs
½ cup cooked and pureed squash
3 scallions, chopped
½ cup cracker crumbs

1 tablespoon Old Bay Seasoning
1 tablespoon lemon juice
7 sheets phyllo dough
Non-stick cooking spray (or melted butter)
¼ cup ground pecans
½ cup shredded Parmesan cheese

Preheat oven to 350°F and grease a 15 inch × 12 inch cookie sheet.

Combine crab, eggs, pureed squash, scallions, cracker crumbs, Old Bay seasoning and lemon juice. Set aside.

Separate first sheet of phyllo and lightly spray or butter. Sprinkle with Parmesan and cover with second sheet of phyllo. Spray and sprinkle with nuts. Alternate cheese and nuts for remaining sheets.

Mold crab mixture in a row on the long edge facing you. Roll all seven sheets to form a tube around crab.

Transfer to pre-greased pan. Bake at 350° 15 to 20 minutes or until golden brown. Cut into 1 inch strudel rolls.

Yield: 6 servings

THREE CHIMNEYS INN

Grilled Sea Scallops

*3 pounds fresh jumbo sea
    scallops
1 tablespoon lemon juice
2 ounces sun dried tomatoes
4 tablespoons minced shallots*

*3 ounces boursin cheese
5 ounces heavy whipping cream
Salt and pepper to taste
2 tablespoons olive oil*

THREE CHIMNEYS
INN

17 Newmarket Rd
Durham, NH 03824

603-868-7800

EMAIL
chimney3@
threechimneysinn.com

URL
www.
threechimneysinn.com

Julienne-cut the sun dried tomatoes.

Add olive oil to a hot skillet and sauté the shallots and julienne sun dried tomatoes until the shallots are translucent.

Add the heavy cream and boursin cheese. Add salt and pepper as needed and reduce sauce until thickened. Remove from heat.

Toss the scallops with the olive oil, lemon juice, and salt and pepper. Grill the scallops until the centers are no longer translucent.

Place the sauce on the bottom of each plate and top it with the grilled scallops.

A further option would be to toss fresh angel hair with the sauce.

THE RED CASTLE INN
HISTORIC LODGINGS

109 Prospect St
Nevada City, CA 95959

530-265-5135

EMAIL
stay@redcastleinn.com

URL
www.redcastleinn.com

THE RED CASTLE INN
HISTORIC LODGINGS

Artichoke Quiche

1 jar marinated artichoke hearts
½ cup onion, chopped
1 clove garlic, minced
4 eggs, slightly beaten
¼ cup bread crumbs, crushed
½ teaspoon salt
¼ teaspoon pepper
½ teaspoon oregano
½ lb. cheddar cheese, grated
2 tablespoons parsley, minced

Preheat oven 350°F.

Drain artichoke hearts, reserving 2 tablespoons of the liquid. Sauté onion and garlic over meduim heat in liquid.

In a large bowl combine eggs, bread crumbs, salt, pepper, and oregano. Coarsely chop artichoke hearts and combine with grated cheddar cheese, and sautéed vegetables.

Combine and turn into greased 9 × 9 baking dish. Sprinkle with minced parsley. Bake at 350°F 30 minutes or until set. Cool and cut into squares.

Yield: 9 servings

JOSHUA GRINDLE INN

Summer Veggi Pie

13 ounces frozen shredded
   potatoes
salt and pepper to taste
1 large onion, sliced thinly
½ cup green onions, chopped
1 tsp garlic, minced
1 Tbsp oil
1½ cups mushrooms, sliced
   thinly

¾ cup broccoli, chopped
1 cup zucchini, sliced
1 lbs extra firm tofu, drained
2 Tbsp oil
2 Tbsp lemon juice
½ tsp garlic powder or granules
1 tsp salt
3 Tbsp flour
paprika

JOSHUA GRINDLE INN

PO Box 647
Mendocino, CA 95460
707-937-4143
EMAIL
stay@joshgrin.com
URL
www.joshgrin.com

More and more these days we have guests who, for health or ethical reasons, are abstaining from animal products. We've been very careful to eliminate meat from all of our dishes, but this request is a little more challenging since we rely so much on milk and eggs in our recipes, especially for the quiches. However, we have found that this quiche is so creamy, tangy and satisfying that no one seems to notice that it is not a 'traditional' quiche.

Oil a glass pie plate and distribute potatoes over bottom of pan. Season with salt and pepper and bake for 20–25 minutes at 350 degrees, stirring occasionally, until slightly browned. Spread softened potatoes evenly over bottom and sides of pans.

Sauté green onions, yellow onions and garlic in oil until tender. Add broccoli, zucchini and mushrooms and sauté until tender. Drain well and place in a large mixing bowl. Set aside.

In food processor, blend tofu, oil, lemon juice, garlic powder, salt and flour until very smooth. Add to vegetable mixture and mix well. Spread mixture evenly into the pie plate. Sprinkle top with paprika. Bake at 350 degrees for 45 minutes until firm and lightly browned on top.

Yield: 12 servings

CASA TIERRA ADOBE
B&B INN

11155 W Calle Pima
Tucson, AZ 85743

520-578-3058

EMAIL
info@casatierratucson.
com

URL
www.casatierratucson.
com

CASA TIERRA ADOBE B & B INN

Casa Tierra Green Chili Polenta

1 cup quick-cooking grits
4 cups water
2 large eggs
1 clove garlic, minced or
*   pressed*
¾ teaspoon pepper
1 teaspoon hot sauce
2 tablespoons butter

½ teaspoon adobo spice
2 cups shredded sharp cheddar
*   cheese*
1 cup diced green chilies
¼ cup red bell pepper
¼ cup green bell pepper
⅓ cup fresh cilantro leaves

Preheat oven to 350°F.

In a 2- to 3-quart pan, blend grits with 4 cups water. Bring to a boil over high heat, stirring often. Add butter. Cover pan and reduce heat to low. Stir often until grits are tender—5 to 6 minutes.

In a large bowl, beat eggs to blend. Stirring, add cheese, chilies, garlic, adobo, pepper and hot sauce to taste. Add grits and pour mixture into a buttered shallow 9 by 13 inch baking dish or 2 ½ to 3 quart casserole.

Bake uncovered in a 350°F oven until lightly browned—40 to 45 minutes. Let stand about 5 minutes. Garnish with red and green bell pepper and cilantro. Cut into into rounds or squares and serve with a wide spatula.

Yield: 7 servings

THE INN AT MANCHESTER
Big Momma's Turkey Hash

THE INN AT
MANCHESTER

3967 Historic Route 7A
Manchester Village,
Vermont 05254
1-800-273-1793

EMAIL

innkeepers@
innatmanchester.com

1 stick of butter
3 tablespoons flour
1 cup chopped onion
Turkey or chicken stock
1 cup red bell pepper, chopped
1 cup green bell pepper, chopped
Salt and pepper to taste
½ tsp. celery seed, more if desired
1 cup chopped potatoes
2 cups chopped turkey

Melt butter in a large skillet, add flour and brown. Add onion and sauté, add 1 cup stock. Add peppers, potatoes, celery seed, and salt and pepper, simmer until potatoes are just soft. Add turkey, heat through. Add more stock, salt and pepper to taste. Serve with jellied cranberry sauce and corn bread.

This is a Southern family favorite.

Yield: 8 servings

Cook Time: 20 min   Prep Time: 10 min

Wood
violets

Side Dishes

Whether you start your meal with a soup and salad or turn your meal into a soup and salad, there are limitless combinations of fresh ingredients to suit your every mood and appetite. Be adventurous and experiment with the many ways to combine vegetables, fruits, meat, and dairies to produce mouth-watering, healthy creations.

The following pages are filled with recipes and ideas that will help you turn a boring pile of lettuce into a delightful hand-tossed mixture of your favorite lettuce, toasted nuts, berries, fruits, fresh vegetables and so much more. Keep your salads healthy and nutritious by making your own dressings and vinaigrettes (and shying away from the store-bought Ranch and Caesar.) Surprise yourself and your family with a homemade soup that did not originate from a can. From thick and hearty bean soups to lighter broths, you'll find soup recipes appropriate for warming up from a chilly day and helping to scare off a bad cold.

Whether you're looking to compliment wines, cheeses, or main dishes, these next several pages are filled with recipes that will inspire you to try innovative taste combinations. Explore how different wines bring out different flavors in your favorite dishes.

Remember that lighter wines are best paired with lighter, spicier foods like fish and chicken; heavier wines nicely compliment richer dishes like steak or a meaty pasta dish. Dive into the world of side dishes to enhance any meal. Find out how to turn plain old broccoli and mashed potatoes into colorful and flavorful accompaniments that will impress and delight your dinner guests. Even desserts can be brought to life with the right accompaniments.

Incorporate fruits, dessert wines, and cheese into your dessert dishes to energize and invigorate the taste buds. Innkeepers have shared their winning accompaniment recipes that have drawn guests back to their dining room table time and time again.

LAMPLIGHT INN B&B
Strawberry Spinach Salad

2 bunches fresh spinach, cleaned and broken into pieces
1½ pints of strawberries, sliced

Dressing:
¾ cup corn oil   *1 teaspoon salt*
⅓ cup fresh lemon juice   *1 teaspoon dried mustard*
½ cup of sugar   *½ teaspoon lemon peel*
1 onion peeled and chopped   *1 tablespoon poppy seeds*

Mix the dressing ingredients together and chill until ready to serve. Pour over spinach and strawberries and toss.

Yield: 8 servings

LAMPLIGHT INN B&B

PO Box 130
Lake Luzerne, NY
12846

518-696-5294

EMAIL
stay@lamplightinn.com

URL
www.lamplightinn.com

LAZY BEE B&B

3651 Deep Lake
Boundary Rd
Colville, WA 99114

509-732-8917

EMAIL
budinger.bender@plix.
com

URL
www.travelguides.
com/home/Lazy_Bee/

L A Z Y   B E E   B & B
Dressed Up Green Salad

Salad:
6 cups salad greens
2 medium navel oranges
1 cup halved red grapes
½ cup golden raisins
¼ cup chopped red onion
¼ cup slided almonds
4 pieces bacon, cooked and crumbled.

Dressing:
½ cup mayonnaise
½ cup honey
¼ cup orange juice
2 tablespoons grated orange peel

In a large bowl, combine salad ingredients.

In another bowl, mix dressing ingredients. Pour over salad, toss and serve.

GLENFIELD PLANTATION
Crunchy Hot Chicken Salad

GLENFIELD
PLANTATION

6 Providence Rd
Natchez, MS 39120

601-442-1002

EMAIL
glenfieldbb@bellsouth.
net

URL
www.
glenfieldplantation.com

3 cups diced chicken, cooked
1 cup finely chopped celery
2 teaspoons chopped onions
½ cup sliced almonds
1 can cream of chicken soup
1½ cups cooked rice
1 tablespoon lemon juice

½ teaspoon salt
¼ teaspoon pepper
¾ cup mayonnaise
¼ cup water
2 eggs
crushed potato chips
¾ cup shredded cheddar cheese

Combine chicken, celery, onions, almonds, cream of chicken soup, cooked rice, lemon juice, salt and pepper. Mix well and set aside.

Combine mayonnaise and water. Beat with a whisk until smooth. Pour over chicken mix and stir well.

Add two eggs and toss gently. Spoon into greased 2-quart, shallow casserole dish. Cover and refrigerate for 8 hours.

Bake at 450 degrees for 10 to 15 minutes and sprinkle with crushed potato chips and cheese.

Bake 5 more minutes.

Yield: 8 servings

SHERWOOD FOREST

Saugatuck, MI 49453

269-857-1246

EMAIL
sf@
sherwoodforestbandb.
com

URL
www.
sherwoodforestbandb.
com

S H E R W O O D   F O R E S T

Ms. Carol's Cool Cucumber Salad

1 cucumber
⅓ cup sugar
⅓ cup cider vinegar
⅓ cup water

Wash and peel cucumber and slice very thin (set aside). Mix sugar, cider vinegar, and water and add cucumber. Refrigerate for 2–3 hours and serve. You can double or triple this delicious dish depending on how big the clan is.

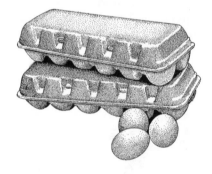

PROSPECT HILL B&B INN

Marie's Warm Potato Salad

1½ lbs. medium size potatoes
    (boiling variety)
½ cup vegetable oil
3 tablespoons flour
1½ cups water
½ cup vinegar (type will affect
    flavor)

2 tablespoons sugar
1¼ teaspoons salt
Pepper to taste
1 egg yolk (or whole egg)
    slightly beaten
1 medium onion, diced
1 cup celery (diced)

Wash potatoes well and cook in boiling salted water until just done. Peel potatoes while warm, slice 1/8 inch thick (about 4 cups).

Meanwhile, mix oil with flour in a pan. Add water and vinegar gradually, stir over medium heat until smooth and thick. Add sugar, salt, and pepper. Stir small amount of hot mixture into the egg then return egg mixture to pan and stir.

Add warm potatoes, onion and celery. Toss lightly by lifting potatoes in and out of dressing. Serve warm.

Yield: 8 servings   Cooking Time: 30 min.

PROSPECT HILL B&B INN

801 W Main St/ Hwy 67
Mountain City, TN 37683

423-727-0139

EMAIL
inn@prospect-hill.com

URL
www.prospect-hill.com

COLUMBIA CITY
HOTEL

Columbia, CA 95310
209-532-1479
EMAIL
esteiness@
foreverresorts.com
URL
www.cityhotel.com

COLUMBIA CITY HOTEL

Asian Chicken Salad

3 heads romaine lettuce, shredded

Dressing:
¼ cup orange juice concentrate
⅓ cup soy sauce
*½ oz ginger, peeled and rough
   chopped*
½ oz garlic, minced
¼ cup cream sherry
½ teaspoon red chili flakes
½ teaspoon mustard powder
2 tablespoons of sesame oil
½ cup canola oil

Optional:
*Grilled chicken breast (serve
   warm or room temp., thinly
   sliced)*
Toasted almonds
Sesame seeds
Fried rice noodles
Tomatoes
Orange or tangerine segments
Snap peas
Water chestnuts

Place all dressing ingredients except oils in blender, run until smooth. Drizzle in oils with blender running.

Toss shredded romaine with dressing, garnish with your choice of the ingredients listed above.

Yield: 6 servings

YELTON MANOR B&B & THE MANOR GUEST HOUSE

Endive Salad With Walnuts

YELTON MANOR B&B
& THE MANOR GUEST
HOUSE

140 North Shore Dr
South Haven, MI 49090

269-637-5220

EMAIL
elaine@yeltonmanor.
com

URL
www.yeltonmanor.com

6 tablespoons olive oil
2 tablespoons minced green
 onion
2 teaspoons Dijon mustard
½ teaspoon sugar
1 Granny Smith apple, peeled,
 cored, and sliced

6 large Belgian Endive,
 separate leaves (wipe, don't
 wash!)
2–3 tablespoons coarsely
 chopped walnuts
2–3 tablespoons finely cubed
 Roquefort cheese
freshly ground pepper

Combine oil, onion, mustard, sugar and apple in a salad bowl and whisk until thoroughly blended. Place the endive leaves into the bowl, then sprinkle with walnuts, cheese and pepper to taste. Chill. Just before serving, toss the salad. Arrange the leaves on a platter or plate and then 'load' them with the mixture.

Yield: 4 servings

EDGEWORTH INN

PO Box 340
Monteagle, TN 37356

931-924-4000

EMAIL
edgeworthinn@charter.
net

URL
www.edgeworthinn.
com

EDGEWORTH INN
Potato Parmesan Soup

8 peeled and chopped potatoes
3 green onions chopped (save
green for garnish)
1 minced garlic clove
1½ tablespoons course ground
pepper

1 tablespoon salt
1 quart heavy cream
1 cup grated parmesan cheese

Boil and puree potatoes. Add chopped white part of green onion, garlic, heavy cream, salt, and pepper. Cook on low heat for 30 minutes. Add parmesan cheese at the end of cook time. Set off burner and allow cheese to melt into soup.

KILAUEA LODGE
Coconut Cream of Celery Soup

KILAUEA LODGE

PO Box 116
Volcano, HI 96785

808-967-7366

EMAIL
stay@kilauealodge.com

URL
www.kilauealodge.com

10 cups chicken broth
3 lbs. Celery stalk—cubed
2 lbs. Russet potato—peeled and cubed
17 oz. milk
½ cup heavy cream
½ cup coconut syrup
1½ tsp. celery stalk
1 tsp. white pepper
8 oz. unsalted butter
Parsley—finely chopped

Add chicken stock in 4 qt. pot. Bring to a boil.

Puree celery and potato in food processor until very fine. Add puree into boiling chicken broth and beat with whip for 2 minutes.

Add milk and heavy cream, and coconut syrup. Stir. Bring to a fast boil, then reduce heat to low and let simmer. Add celery salt and white pepper. Stir.

Cover pot and let simmer for 40 minutes. Stir frequently. Remove pot from stove. With a 2 oz. ladle force liquid through a fine sift into a 4 qt. Bowl.

Discard heavy puree in sift. Cut butter into ½ inch cubes. Add to cream of celery in the bowl.

Whip until butter has dissolved. Sprinkle a little parsley on each serving.

SUNSET HILL HOUSE -
A GRAND INN

231 Sunset Hill Rd
Sugar Hill, NH 03586

603-823-5522

EMAIL
innkeeper@
sunsethillhouse.com

URL
www.sunsethillhouse.
com

SUNSET HILL HOUSE – A GRAND INN

Creamy Pumpkin Soup

*1 medium pumpkin, poached &
    peeled, or one large can of
    pumpkin puree if you're in
    a pinch!*
*¼ pound butter, 1 stick, cut
    into small pieces*
1 cup onion, diced
1 cup celery, diced

½ cup all-purpose flour
1 cup sherry
2 quarts chicken stock
3 cups cream
*¼ cup New Hampshire maple
    syrup*
Salt & pepper to taste

Poach and peel pumpkin and reserve. Add butter to a soup pan
and melt. Add onion and sauté until translucent. Add celery
and sauté. Add flour and form roux. Add sherry and de-glaze
pan. Add chicken stock; bring to a boil while mixing. Drop to a
simmer. Add pumpkin, maple syrup, salt & pepper and blend.
Add cream, stir and serve.

B R I G H T W O O D   G U E S T H O U S E

Grandma Hinson's Potato Soup

⅓ cup of butter
1 medium yellow (sweet) onion,
    peeled and diced (use 2
    onions if you like a lot)
3 stalks of celery, diced (include
    the leafy tops)
2 or 3 carrots, diced
1 teaspoon salt
1 teaspoon pepper
2 tablespoons flour
1 cup of milk

6 cups of water
5 potatoes, cubed (about 1-inch
    pieces)
4 veggie or chicken bouillon
    cubes
2 tablespoons parsley, chopped
    (or use dried flakes)
Other herbs such as savory,
    thyme, marjoram, chives,
    as desired

Melt 2 tablespoons butter (or use 1 tablespoon vegetable oil) in a large skillet over medium heat. Add salt, pepper, onion, celery and carrots and sauté until just soft, and their aroma is released.

In a small bowl or 2-cup glass measuring cup, blend the flour and milk with a fork. Set aside.

Put the water and potatoes in a large pot. Add the bouillon cubes. Add the sautéed veggies, and the remaining butter. Cook over medium heat, until potatoes are soft but not too mushy, about 10–15 minutes. Check it often, stirring gently. Add the fresh or dried herbs.

Blend the milk and flour again, making sure the lumps are gone. Add to the soup, and stir until thickened and heated through.

Serve with bread and butter.

Yield: 6 servings

Cooking Time: 30 min.

BRIGHTWOOD GUESTHOUSE

PO Box 189
Brightwood, OR 97011

503-622-5783

EMAIL
brightwoodbnb@
hotmail.com

URL
www.Mounthoodbnb.
com

GOLDEN PHEASANT
INN

763 River Rd
Erwinna, PA 18920

610-294-9595

EMAIL
barbara@
goldenpheasant.com

URL
www.goldenpheasant.
com

GOLDEN PHEASANT INN

Spicy Pumpkin Bisque

½ cup butter
2 cups onion, chopped
1 cup celery, chopped
6 garlic cloves, minced
8 cups vegetable or chicken
 stock
2 cups tomatoes, chopped
4 bay leaves

1 teaspoon nutmeg, freshly
 grated
1 teaspoon cayenne pepper
4 cups pumpkin puree
2 cups heavy cream
Salt and pepper
¼ cup Italian parsley, chopped

Melt the butter in a large stockpot. Add onions, celery and garlic and sauté until onions are clear.

Add stock, tomatoes, bay leaves, nutmeg and cayenne pepper. Bring to boil. Reduce heat to a simmer and cover. Cook until vegetables are very soft, about 20 minutes.

Strain and reserve the liquid. In a food processor or blender, puree the vegetables with some of the liquid. Strain through a sieve.

In the stockpot, combine the remaining liquid, pureed vegetables and pumpkin. Heat through while stirring, about 10 minutes. Add cream. Season with salt and pepper.

Heat through while stirring, about 5 minutes. Garnish with parsley. Serve.

Yield: 7 servings

CAPTAIN FREEMAN INN

Winter Squash Gratin

CAPTAIN FREEMAN
INN

15 Breakwater Rd
Brewster, MA 02631

508-896-7481

EMAIL
stay@
captainfreemaninn.com

URL
www.
captainfreemaninn.com

2 lbs. winter squash, like
  butternut, acorn, or blue
  Hubbard
½ cup rice boiled for 10 min
  and drained well
1 cup grated Gruyere cheese
4 tablespoon flour

3 cloves of garlic, finely
  chopped
5 tablespoon fresh thyme, finely
  chopped
½ teaspoon nutmeg
salt and pepper
4 oz. fresh bread crumbs
olive oil

Preheat oven to 325°F.

Toss all the ingredients except the bread crumbs and oil until the squash is well coated. Put in a well oiled gratin or casserole dish and cover with bread crumbs. Drizzle with oil and bake at 325 degrees until deep caramel brown.

MOUNTAIN BROOK
COTTAGES

208 Mountain Brook
Rd #18
Sylva, NC 28779

828-586-4329

EMAIL
mcmahon@
mountainbrook.com

URL
www.mountainbrook.
com

MOUNTAIN BROOK COTTAGES

Spinach 'Brownies'

2 bags fresh spinach (chopped)
   OR 1 10-oz package of
   frozen spinach
1 cup all purpose flour
1 teaspoon salt
1 teaspoon baking powder
2 teaspoons onion powder
1 teaspoon garlic powder (NOT
   garlic salt)

½ teaspoon red pepper flakes
   (you can omit pepper flakes
   if you don't like them)
2 eggs
1 cup milk
½ cup melted butter
1 chopped onion
1 8-oz block of Cabot Cheddar
   Cheese (seriously sharp,
   Hunter's favorite) shredded

Preheat oven to 375 degrees. Grease 9 × 13 pan. Thoroughly mix all ingredients together in a bowl. Pour in pan and bake for 30 to 35 minutes or until golden brown. Let cool 15 or more minutes before serving. For an even tastier treat, add more shredded Cabot Cheddar Cheese on top and/or feta cheese. This dish is good for breakfast, lunch or dinner, and it is even better the next day as leftovers!

Yield: 6 servings

AUBERGE MAISON VIENNEAU INN

Mushroom Potatoes a la Marie

AUBERGE MAISON
VIENNEAU INN

426 Main St
Shediac, NB E4P 2G4
Canada

506-532-5412

EMAIL
info@maisonvienneau.
com

URL
www.maisonvienneau.
com/

Small brown, red or white baby potatoes
Steak spice or Mrs. Dash (Montreal steak spice preferred)

Take an apple corer with a handle and insert in one end of potato and twist. Take a small knife and cut on the cylinder at the top all around and remove "donut" (use for another purpose). What is left will look like a stem atop a mushroom cap.

Cook in salted water—cover for 15 minutes until just tender (do not overcook). Drain and refrigerate overnight to firm up. Must be cold.

In a wide frying pan, melt butter just enough to cover the bottom (1–2 teaspoons). Add potatoes. Heat over medium until hot. Sprinkle with steak spice or Mrs. Dash. Shake pan to turn and brown. Do not overcook.

Serve with dinner or breakfast.

1859 HISTORIC
NATIONAL HOTEL &
RESTAURANT

PO Box 502
Jamestown, CA 95327

209-984-3446

EMAIL
info@national-hotel.
com

URL
www.national-hotel.
com

1859 HISTORIC NATIONAL HOTEL & RESTAURANT

Tequila Kiwi Lime Salsa

6 kiwis (peeled and diced)
1 small red onion (finely chopped)
1 small bunch of cilantro (finely chopped)
5 limes (squeezed)
½ tomato (finely chopped)
2 ounces Tequila

Combine all ingredients together in a bowl. Cover and store in the refrigerator until ready to serve.

Comments:
The next time you are planning to prepare a Halibut, Mahi-Mahi, Salmon, Sea bass, Swordfish or even tuna, serve it with some of this salsa. Your guests are sure to be delighted.

Yield: 3 servings

Desserts

A well-crafted dessert is not just the final touch to a fine meal; it can be the beginning of a wonderful evening. Dessert making is an art that innkeepers throughout North America have taken to new heights. They are masters of entertaining, so why not benefit from their expertise when that special occasion comes along. Choose from a variety of extravagant and seasonal sweets.

CAPTAIN'S INN AT
MOSS LANDING

PO Box 570
Moss Landing, CA
95039

831-633-5550

EMAIL
res@captainsinn.com
URL
www.captainsinn.com

CAPTAIN'S INN AT MOSS LANDING

Double Chocolate Oatmeal Cookies

Mix Wet (A)
1½ cups white sugar
1 cup butter
1 egg
½ cup water
1 Teaspoon vanilla

Add Dry and Mix (B)
1½ cups flour
⅓ cup powdered baking cocoa
½ teaspoon baking soda
½ teaspoon salt

Add Last and Mix (C)
3 cups old fashioned oatmeal
6 ounces semisweet chocolate chips
¼ cup pecans

Pre-heat oven to 350°F.

Mix group A (sugar, butter, egg, vanilla) in a large mixing bowl. Mix group B (flour, cocoa, soda, salt) in a separate mixing bowl. Add group B to bowl with Group A, mix until well blended.

To this dough add group C (oats, chocolate chips, nuts) and mix well. Chill finished dough mix for one hour. Roll dough into balls (about 2 Tablespoons per ball) and place on no-stick cookie sheet. Bake at 350°F for 10–12 minutes. Be sure to have plenty of cold milk on hand when serving.

Yield: 20 servings

Cooking Time: 10 min.

LILY CREEK LODGE
Arvilla's Rice Pudding

LILY CREEK LODGE

2608 Auraria Rd
Dahlonega, GA 30533

706-864-6848

EMAIL
lilycreeklodge@
windstream.net

URL
www.lilycreeklodge.
com

2 large eggs
½ cup sugar
1 tsp. vanilla
2 cups milk
2 cups precooked rice

1 tbsp. butter, melted
½ cup raisins (or more)
Nutmeg

Preheat oven to about 325 degrees F.

Combine eggs, sugar and vanilla. Add ½ cup milk and stir. Repeat adding milk and stirring four times till milk is used. Add cooled, melted butter. Pour mixture into rice. Add raisins. Sprinkle nutmeg on top.

Bake 1 hour or until knife inserted into middle comes out clean.

Yield: 6 servings

Cooking Time: 1 hr

CASTLE MARNE B&B

1572 Race St
Denver, CO 80206

303-331-0621

EMAIL
info@castlemarne.com

URL
www.castlemarne.com

C A S T L E   M A R N E   B & B

Chocolate Shortbread

1 cup all-purpose flour	1 stick of butter, softened
⅛ teaspoon salt	½ cup sugar
2 tablespoons corn starch	½ teaspoon vanilla
1 heaping teaspoon baking cocoa	¼ teaspoon almond extract
	Chocolate sprinkles

In small bowl mix flour, salt, corn starch and baking cocoa together, set aside. In medium mixing bowl, beat softened butter with electric mixer until smooth. Add sugar and beat a little while longer. Add vanilla and almond extract and beat. Add the dry ingredients to butter mixture and cut it in with a pastry cutter until thoroughly mixed. Gather into a ball and press into pie pan. Use a thin knife to draw the dough slightly away from the edges. Make a decoration on the dough by pressing the tines of a fork into it. Mark with a knife into 16–18 wedges. Sprinkle with chocolate sprinkles. Bake in center pre-heated oven 20 min., then turn and bake 20 min. longer. DO NOT OVERCOOK! Remove from oven and allow the shortbread to cool for approximately 10 min. Gently re-score with a sharp knife to cut wedges.

Yield: 16 servings

A A R O N   S H I P M A N   H O U S E
B & B

Apple Cinnamon Coffee Ring

Dough:
1 cup milk
⅓ cup sugar
1 package dry yeast
¼ cup warm water
½ teaspoon salt
2 eggs
⅓ cup butter
4½–5 cups all purpose flour

Filling:
1 cup delicious apples
½ cup brown sugar
1 teaspoon cinnamon
1 tsp grated orange peel
1 tsp vanilla
½ cup chopped pecans

Glaze:
¾ cup confectioners' sugar
1 tbsp orange juice
*For glaze, just mix orange juice
    and confectioner's together.*

AARON SHIPMAN
HOUSE B&B

Washington, DC 20009
413-582-9888

EMAIL
reservations@
bedandbreakfastdc.com

URL
www.
aaronshipmanhouse.
com

Dissolve yeast in water. Set aside until foamy. Meanwhile, heat milk, sugar, butter and salt in a small saucepan to 110 degrees. In a separate bowl combine milk, yeast, flour and eggs and stir until it forms a soft dough. Turn out onto a floured surface and knead dough 5 minutes or until elastic. Oil a large bowl, place dough in bowl, cover and let rise in a warm place about 1 hour.

Meanwhile, sauté apples with vanilla in butter until soft. Remove from heat and add brown sugar, cinnamon, orange peel and pecans. Mix well and set aside.

When dough has risen, roll out on floured surface to an 11 × 9 inch rectangle. Brush with remaining 2 tablespoons melted butter and top with apple mixture, leaving ½ inch border at edges. Fold dough in thirds lengthwise to make 11 × 3 inch roll. Cut crosswise into 12 equal pieces. Arrange pieces, cut side up, in greased 9 inch springform pan forming a ring. Cover and let rise 40 minutes. Preheat oven to 325 degrees. Bake coffee cake 30–35 minutes or until golden brown. Cool on wire rack. Remove from pan and drizzle glaze over the ring and serve.

MANSION HOUSE B&B AND SPA

Mansion House Rum Walnut Cake

MANSION HOUSE B&B
AND SPA

105 5th Ave NE
St. Petersburg, FL 33701

727-821-9391

EMAIL
mansion1@ix.netcom.
com

URL
www.mansionbandb.
com

1 cup chopped walnuts
Yellow or Chocolate cake mix
    with pudding in it
3 large eggs
⅓ cup vegetable oil
½ cup cold water
½ cup dark rum, 80 proof

Glaze:
1 stick of unsalted butter
¼ cup water
1 cup granulated sugar
½ cup dark rum

Preheat the oven to 325 degrees. Grease and flour a 10 inch tube or 12-cup bundt pan. Sprinkle the nuts over the bottom of the pan. Mix all of the cake incredients together until wet. Beat with a mixer for 2 minutes at medium speed. Pour the batter over the nuts and bake for one (1) hour.

Cool the cake on a rack for 20 minutes and then remove it from the pan. When it is cool, invert it, nutty side up, on a serving dish. Poke holes into the cake with a long fork (I use a carving fork).

Prepare the glaze for the cake:

Melt the butter in a sauce pan. Sir in the water and sugar. Boil for five (5) minutes sirring constantly. Remove the pan from the heat and stir in the rum.

Spoon and brush the glaze over the top of the cake until it is absorbed. Repeat until it is used up.

THE RICHARDS HOUSE
Pumpkin Roll

THE RICHARDS
HOUSE

1492 Locust St
Dubuque, IA 52001

563-557-1492

EMAIL
innkeeper@
therichardshouse.com

URL
www.therichardshouse.
com

3 eggs
1 cup sugar
⅔ cup pumpkin puree
1 teaspoon lemon juice
¾ cup flour
1 teaspoon baking powder
½ teaspoon salt
½ teaspoon nutmeg
1½ teaspoons cinnamon

Filling:
1 cup powdered sugar
8 ounces cream cheese (room temperature)
4 tablespoons butter or margarine
½ teaspoon vanilla

Mix together as listed. Line 1½ inch by 15 inch cookie sheet with waxed paper. Trim excess waxed paper to minimize smoking. Pour batter onto cookie sheet, spread evenly. Bake 12–15 minutes at 375 degrees. (May sprinkle with nuts before baking.)

Prepare linen towel heavily sprinkled with powdered sugar. After baking, turn onto towel, waxed paper side up. Remove paper and roll into towel. Cool 30–40 minutes rolled. Prepare filling while roll cools. Mix ingredients thoroughly. After roll has cooled, unroll and spread filling evenly. Re-roll. Slice for serving.

Yield: 8 servings

HAWTHORNE INN

462 Lexington Rd
Concord, MA 01742

978-369-5610

EMAIL
inn@concordmass.com

URL
www.concordmass.com

HAWTHORNE INN
Morning Cake Delight

1 lb. butter
6 eggs
½ cup sour cream
½ cup milk
1½ teaspoons almond extract
1 tablespoon baking powder
2 cups sugar
1 banana
4 cups flour
1 cup berries

Hawthorne Inn Topping:
½ cup freshly whipped cream
½ cup fruited yogurt
½ cup sour cream

Mix first 8 ingredients extremely well until a smooth consistency is reached. Beat in the flour until well coated but do not overbeat. Pour ½ of mixture into pan, add a layer of berries, pour the rest of the mixture in.

Bake at 375 degrees for 1¼ hours in a buttered and floured Bundt pan. Serve with Hawthorne Inn Topping.

Topping: Fold yogurt and sour cream into whipped cream and serve.

Yield: 8 servings

BREAKFAST ON THE CONNECTICUT

Chocolate Fondue

2 Tbsp. sugar
1 cup heavy cream
8 ounces chopped bittersweet chocolate
1 Tbsp. butter
1 Tbsp. cabernet sauvignon

In a microwave safe bowl combine sugar, heavy cream, chocolate and butter. Microwave for 2 minutes. Take out of microwave and give it a quick whisk. Add wine and whisk again. Transfer to fondue pot with a low flame underneath. Serve with pound cake, strawberries or biscotti bits.

Easy and so much fun!

BREAKFAST ON THE
CONNECTICUT

651 River Rd
Lyme, NH 03768

603-353-4444

EMAIL
breakfast.connecticut@
valley.net

URL
www.breakfastonthect.
com

THE CHALET INN

285 Lone Oak Dr
Dillsboro, NC 28789

828-586-0251

EMAIL
paradisefound@
chaletinn.com

URL
www.chaletinn.com

THE CHALET INN

Apfelküchen

11 oz self-rising flour
8 oz sugar
5 oz butter
2 egg yolks
pinch salt
1 lb cooking apples (or drained,
    canned apples)
juice of 1 lemon
pinch of cinnamon

2 oz raisins
2 oz ground hazelnuts
2 oz ground almonds
2 Tbsp apricot jam
2 oz vanilla icing (homemade or
    canned)
2 Tbsp cherry liquor

Sift flour into a bowl. Stir in 5 oz of the sugar and kneed in the butter. Add egg yolks and salt, and mix to a smooth dough. Chill for 20 minutes. Roll out half of the dough to cover the bottom of a 9½ inch by 3 inch high Spring Form Pan. Bake at 400 degrees F for 15 minutes.

Peel, core and slice the apples and mix with remaining sugar. Add lemon juice, cinnamon, raisins and nuts. Moisten with a little water to blend.

Spoon evenly onto the baked pastry shell still in the Spring Form Pan. Roll out the remaining dough and cover the filling (you can also make decorative strips to cover the filling). Bake in preheated oven for 30 minutes. Cool in the Spring Form Pan overnight. An hour before serving, remove from Spring Form Pan and allow the cake to reach room temperature. Shortly before serving, warm the jam and spread over the cake. Combine the icing and cherry liquor (e.g. Kirsch) and dribble over the jam.

Yield: 6 servings

CASTLE   MARNE   B & B

Castle Marne's Chocolate Truffles

CASTLE MARNE B&B

1572 Race St
Denver, CO 80206

303-331-0621

EMAIL
info@castlemarne.com

URL
www.castlemarne.com

1 cup semisweet chocolate chips
2 squares (1 oz. each)
    unsweetened chocolate,
    chopped
1½ cups powdered sugar
½ cup butter, softened

2 tbsp. B&B Liqueur (orange,
    raspberry, hazelnut, or
    other flavored liqueurs may
    be used)

Melt the chocolate chips and unsweetened chocolate in a heavy, small saucepan over low heat, stirring constantly. Set aside and let chocolate cool slightly.

Combine the powdered sugar, butter, and liqueur in a bowl. Beat with an electric mixer. Beat in the cooled chocolate until smooth. Refrigerate about 30 minutes or until the mixture is fudgy and can be shaped into balls.

Shape the mixture into 1 inch balls by rolling in the palms of your hands. Then roll the truffles in chocolate sprinkles, cocoa, chopped nuts or cookie crumbs to add flavor and prevent the truffles from melting in your fingers. You can also try drizzling melted milk chocolate over the rolled truffles for a pretty effect.

Yield: 2 dozen

HACIENDA
NICHOLAS B&B

320 E Marcy St
Santa Fe, NM 87501

505-992-8385

EMAIL
info@haciendanicholas.
com

URL
www.haciendanicholas.
com

HACIENDA NICHOLAS B&B

Mounds Balls

1 cup softened butter
1 cup milk
3 to 4 cups semi-sweet chocolate chips
2–3 squares unsweetened chocolate
1–2 cups white chocolate chips
8 cups powdered sugar
12 cups shredded coconut

In a double boiler melt semi-sweet and unsweetened chocolate. Meanwhile, in a large bowl mix together butter, sugar, milk and coconut. Form into 1–2 inch balls. (If batter is too soft put it in the freezer for 10–15 minutes.) Then with the ball of coconut mix resting on a fork, dip it into the melted chocolate, set on wax paper and chill.

After chocolate is hardened, melt the white chocolate in a small ziplock plastic bag in the microwave. Check after 45 seconds.

Squish the chips and stir a bit in the bag. Continue cooking for an additional 30 seconds or until completely melted, in 30 second intervals.

Let cool for a minute. Then snip the very end of a corner of the bag and drizzle on the balls. Let chocolate harden on own or chill, then serve.

You may opt to use only half the coconut mix and freeze the rest for later use.

Yield: 6 dozen

GREENVILLE ARMS 1889
INN

Pumpkin Cheesecake with Praline Topping

Cheesecake
1½ pounds (3 8-ounce
    packages) cream cheese
1 cup light brown sugar
¼ cup sour cream
5 eggs
1 15-ounce can pumpkin
1 tablespoon cornstarch
½ tablespoon cinnamon
½ teaspoon ginger
½ teaspoon cloves
1 tablespoon dark rum

Topping
½ cup pecans
⅓ cup brown sugar
1½ ounces butter
Whipped cream if desired to top

GREENVILLE ARMS
1889 INN

PO Box 659
Greenville, NY 12083

518-966-5219

EMAIL
stay@greenvillearms.
com

URL
www.greenvillearms.
com

Preheat oven to 350 degrees.

Butter or grease with shortening a 10 inch springform pan. Line it with greased baking parchment paper.

Mix the cheesecake ingredients in the order given and beat until smooth. Pour into the prepared pan. Bake in a hot water bath for about 1 hour, or until almost set.

Combine the topping ingredients and process in a food processor until blended. Spread on top of cheesecake and bake an additional 20 minutes until the topping is bubbly brown.

Turn the oven off and leave the cake in it for about an hour. Cool on a table until it is room temperature, then chill thoroughly in the refrigerator. Remove from pan when ready to serve, slice and top with whipped cream.

The ingredients may be doubled to make two cakes.

Yield: 8 servings

Cooking Time: 1 hr 20 min

L'AUBERGE
PROVENCALE

PO Box 190
White Post, VA 22620

540-837-1375

EMAIL
info@
laubergeprovencale.
com

URL
www.
laubergeprovencale.
com

L ' A U B E R G E   P R O V E N C A L E

Provencale Orange Blossom Cookie - Oreilletes

1 lb. flour
¼ cup sugar
3 eggs—beaten
1 lemon peel
1 orange peel
¼ cup orange flower water

2 Tbsp butter—softened
1 pinch salt
1 cup lite oil for frying
confectioners sugar

Shred lemon and orange peel with grater. Mix with flour, softened butter, sugar, orange water, eggs and salt. Knead the dough adding a little water if necessary. Cover and let stand for 2 hours.

Roll out dough onto floured surface ¼ inch thick. Cut dough into 4 inch squares. Heat oil in frying pan until very hot. Fry oreilletes. When they are golden, remove and drain. Sprinkle with confectioners sugar.

Cooking Time: 30 min.

A B E L L A   G A R D E N   I N N   B & B

Italian Biscotti

ABELLA GARDEN INN
B&B

210 Oak St
Arroyo Grande, CA
93420

805-489-5926

EMAIL
info@abellagardeninn.
com

URL
www.abellagardeninn.
com

2 cups flour
1 cup sugar
1 teaspoon baking powder
¼ teaspoon baking soda
⅛ teaspoon salt
3 tablespoons butter, at room
    temperature

2 eggs
1 egg yolk
1 teaspoon vanilla
2 teaspoons freshly grated
    orange peel
1 cup chopped almonds

Preheat oven to 350 degrees F.

In a large mixing bowl, combine the first 6 ingredients. In a separate bowl, combine the remaining ingredients (except for the almonds), and lightly beat with a fork until blended.

Add the egg mixture to the flour mixture and beat with a hand-held mixer at medium speed until dough forms. (if it's too stiff for your mixer, only mix until it is a rough mass, and then knead it with flour-dusted hands until all the ingredients are well mixed.)

Add the almonds and mix well. Turn the dough out on a lightly floured board and knead for 1 minute. Divide the dough into 4 equal portions. Using the palms of your hands, roll each portion into a log about 12 inches long and 1 inch in diameter.

Butter a 12-inch wide baking sheet, spacing them about 2 inches apart. Using the palm of your hand, lightly flatten the top of each log until it is about ½ inch thick.

Bake the logs in the top ⅔ of the oven until golden brown, 15–20 minutes. Remove from the oven and let cool on the baking sheet. Leave oven set at 350 degrees. Transfer the logs to a cutting board and cut them crosswise on the diagonal into pieces ½ inch wide. Arrange the pieces' cut sides down back on the baking sheet. Return to oven and bake until lightly toasted and the edges are golden brown, 10 minutes. Let cool before serving.

Yield: 8 servings

Cooking Time: 30 min.

BRACKENRIDGE
HOUSE

230 Madison
San Antonio, TX 78204

210-271-3442

EMAIL
brackenridgebb@aol.
com

URL
www.
brackenridgehouse.
com/

BRACKENRIDGE HOUSE
Brackenridge House Brownies

5 large eggs
3 cups sugar
1½ cups canola oil
1¾ cups flour
6 tablespoons cocoa
½ teaspoon salt
1 tablespoon vanilla
4 cups chopped pecans or walnuts

Beat together the eggs and sugar until thick and lemon colored. Add the oil and beat well. Add the flour, cocoa, salt and vanilla and beat. Stir in chopped nuts.

Spray a 15 × 11 inch jelly roll pan with cooking spray. Pour batter into pan and bake at 350 degrees for 30–45 minutes, until a knife inserted into the center comes out clean.

Cool before cutting. No need for baking powder or baking soda in this recipe.

BAY BREEZE B&B COTTAGES

Addicting Chocolate Chip Cookies

BAY BREEZE B&B
COTTAGES

5660 S Double Bluff Rd
Freeland, WA 98249

360-321-4277

EMAIL
stay@
baybreezecottages.com

URL
www.
baybreezecottages.com

1 cup butter
1½ cups light brown sugar
1 egg
2 teaspoons vanilla
2 cups flour
1 teaspoon baking soda
1 teaspoon cinnamon
1 or 2 teaspoons chopped candied ginger
½ teaspoon salt
1 12-ounce package chocolate chips
1 cup chopped pecans
Reserve: 1 cup powdered sugar

Cream butter, add brown sugar, egg and vanilla. Mix flour, baking soda, ginger, salt and cinnamon. Blend into buttermix. Stir in chocolate chips and nuts.

Chill until firm. Roll dough into 1-inch balls and dredge in powdered sugar.

Put on lightly greased cookie sheets 2 inches apart. Bake at 375°F for 9–10 minutes, don't let them get too brown, just set. Cool 5 minutes and then remove to cooling rack.

Yield: 6 dozen

THE QUEEN VICTORIA
B&B

102 Ocean St
Cape May, NJ 08204

609-884-8702

EMAIL
stay@queenvictoria.
com

URL
www.queenvictoria.
com

THE   QUEEN   VICTORIA   B & B

Chocolate Revel Bars

1 cup margarine or butter,
*   softened*
2½ cups flour
2 cups brown sugar
2 eggs
4 teaspoons vanilla
1 teaspoon baking soda

3 cups oatmeal
1½ cups chocolate chips
1 14-ounce can sweetened
*   condensed milk*
2 tablespoons margarine or
*   butter*
½ cup chopped walnuts

In a large mixer bowl, beat 1 cup margarine until creamy. Add half the flour, brown sugar, eggs, 2 teaspoons vanilla and soda. Beat until thoroughly combined. Beat in remaining flour and oatmeal. Cook chocolate chips, condensed milk and 2 tablespoons margarine over low heat until chocolate is melted, stirring occasionally. Remove from heat and stir in remaining vanilla and nuts. Pat ⅔ of oat mixture into bottom of ungreased 15 inch × 10 inch × 1 inch rimmed cookie sheet. Spread chocolate mixture on top. Dot with remaining oat mixture.

Bake at 350°F about 25 minutes or until top is lightly golden. Cool and cut into bars.

Yield: 5 dozen

A B & B AT DARTMOUTH HOUSE

Raspberry Fudge Truffle Bars

A B&B AT
DARTMOUTH HOUSE

215 Dartmouth St
Rochester, NY 14607

585-271-7872

EMAIL
stay@dartmouthhouse.
com

URL
www.dartmouthhouse.
com

Bottom Layer:
½ cup butter or margarine
1⅓ cups semisweet chocolate chips
2 eggs
¾ cup packed brown sugar
1 teaspoon instant coffee crystals, dissolved in: 1 teaspoon boiling water
½ teaspoon baking powder
¾ cup all-purpose flour

Filling:
1 cup (6 ounce) semisweet chocolate chips

1 package (8 ounce) cream cheese, softened
⅓ cup confectioners' sugar
⅓ cup seedless red raspberry jam (⅓ cup of seeded jam forced through a strainer equals ⅓ cup seedless)
Optional: 1 teaspoon raspberry flavoring

Topping:
1 teaspoon vegetable shortening
¼ cup semisweet chocolate chips

Preheat oven to 350°. Grease a 9 inch square pan.

Bottom Layer: Melt butter and chocolate chips in a heavy pan over low heat, or microwave on medium low. Microwave 1 minute and stir every 30 seconds until melted. Cool slightly.

Beat eggs & brown sugar with electric mixer until well blended and smooth, about 1 minute. Dissolve coffee crystals in hot water before combining with egg mixture. Add melted chocolate chips and mix well. Stir baking powder and flour together before adding and mixing. Spread evenly in a greased 9 inch square baking pan. Bake for 30 to 35 min. or until bars test done. Cool.

Filling: Melt chocolate chips and cool. Beat cream cheese until fluffy and add confectioners' sugar, jam and flavoring. Stir in melted chocolate and spread over the cooled bars.

Topping: Melt shortening and chocolate chips together and drizzle over the filling. To drizzle, put melted mixture in a small plastic bag. Snip a tiny bit off from one corner and squeeze out chocolate to drizzle. Refrigerate before cutting. Store tightly covered in the refrigerator.

Yield: 5 dozen

4-1/2 STREET INN

55 4-1/2 St
Highlands, NC 28741

828-526-4464

EMAIL
relax@4andahalfstinn.
com

URL
www.4andahalfstinn.
com

4 ½ STREET INN

Famous 4½ Street Inn Cookies

1 cup butter
1¼ cups packed brown sugar
½ cup granulated sugar
2 eggs
2 Tbsp. milk
2 tsp. vanilla
1¾ cups unbleached all purpose flour
1 tsp. baking soda
½ tsp. salt
2½ cups oatmeal
2 cups Chocoate Chips (12 oz. package)
1 cup slivered almonds
1 cup coconut

Pre-heat oven to 350 degrees. Beat butter and sugar untill creamy. Add eggs, milk, and vanilla. Combine four, baking soda, and salt. Add dry ingredients to butter mixture. Stir in oats, chips, nuts, and coconuts.

Bake for 8 minutes.

Yield: 3 dozen

1870 WEDGWOOD BED & BREAKFAST INN OF NEW HOPE, PA

Wedding Cookies

1 cup butter or margarine,
   softened
½ cup powdered sugar
2 cups flour

⅛ teaspoon salt
½ teaspoon vanilla

Add powdered sugar to softened butter and mix until smooth. Add flour, salt and vanilla to mixture and cream together. Mixture should be stiff. Roll dough into balls and bake at 400 degrees for 10 to 12 minutes. Roll cookies in powdered sugar before cooling.

Yield: 3 dozen

1870 WEDGWOOD BED & BREAKFAST INN OF NEW HOPE, PA

111 W Bridge St
New Hope, PA 18938

215-862-2570

EMAIL
stay@wedgwoodinn.com

URL
www.WedgwoodInn.com

WILLIAMSBURG
SAMPLER B&B INN

922 Jamestown Rd
Williamsburg, VA 23185

757-253-0398

EMAIL
info@
williamsburgsampler.
com

URL
www.
williamsburgsampler.
com

WILLIAMSBURG SAMPLER
B & B INN

Lazy Chocolate Cookies

(No Bake)
2 cups sugar
½ cup water
½ cup cocoa
4 tablespoon butter (margarine
   substitute OK)

1 teaspoon salt
½ cup peanut butter
1 teaspoon vanilla
3 cups uncooked quick oats

Combine sugar, water, cocoa, butter and salt in saucepan. Boil for about one minute. Add peanut butter, vanilla and oatmeal. Cool slightly. Form into 1-inch balls and let cool completely.

Yield: 6 dozen

WINTERWOOD AT PETERSHAM

Fudge Brownies

½ cup butter
2 squares unsweetened chocolate
1 cup sugar
2 cups flour
½ cup chocolate chips
2 eggs
1 teaspoon vanilla
1 cup miniature marshmallows

Preheat oven to 350 degrees. Melt butter, chocolate, and chocolate chips in the top of a double boiler. Set aside. Beat eggs well until thick and lemon colored.

Add sugar slowly while beating mixture. When smooth, stir in melted chocolate/butter mixture. Stir in vanilla. Fold in flour in small amounts until well blended. Batter will be stiff.

Add marshmallows, blend well. Bake in a greased 8-inch square pan for 25–30 minutes. Cut when cool into bars.

Serve with a scoop of coffee ice cream and hot fudge sauce.

Yield: 7 servings

WINTERWOOD AT PETERSHAM

PO Box 176
Petersham, MA 01366

978-724-8885

EMAIL
winterwood
atpetersham@verizon.
net

URL
www.winterwoodinn.
net

FOUNTAIN HALL

609 S East St
Culpeper, VA 22701

540-825-8200

EMAIL
visit@fountainhall.com

URL
www.fountainhall.com

FOUNTAIN HALL

Grandma Paterno's Holiday Tea Cookies

½ cup sugar
5 cups flour
3½ teaspoons baking powder
7 eggs
½ cup oil
grated orange peel to taste
pinch of salt
½ teaspoon vanilla

Mix flour, sugar, baking powder and salt together. Add eggs, orange peel, vanilla and oil. Mix well. Roll into logs approximately ¾ inch thick and approximately 4–6 inch long. Pinch ends of logs together, forming a crescent shape.

Bake at 350 for approximately 20 minutes or until light brown. Let cool, then dip in icing:

Icing:
Mix confectioner's sugar and fresh lemon juice together (the mixture should be thick like molasses). Dip the top of each cookie in icing and add a shake of candy sprinkles.

Let cool and enjoy!

P O R T O B E L L O   I N N

Lucious Banana Ice Cream

PORTOBELLO INN

PO Box 169
Herkimer, NY 13350

315-823-8612

EMAIL
stay@portobelloinn.com

URL
www.portobelloinn.
com

*4 ripe bananas, peeled &
   mashed*
*1 14-oz. can sweetened
   condensed milk (Carnation)*

2 cup whipping cream

In a large bowl, combine bananas, condensed milk and heavy cream and whisk together until smooth. Pour the banana mixture into an 9 inch × 13 inch × 2 inch baking dish or a large stainless bowl. Cover with plastic wrap and freeze until softly set, stirring occasionally. This should take about 2 hours or so.

Transfer the semi-frozen banana mixture to a large bowl using an electric hand mixer or your stand mixer. Beat the ice cream until fluffy. Return to the same glass dish, cover and freeze until firm (about 6 hours). This can be made ahead. Great with desserts that are complemented by the flavor of banana. Serves 12.

Yield: 12 servings

THE INN AT 410

410 N Leroux St
Flagstaff, AZ 86001

928-774-0088

EMAIL
info@inn410.com

URL
www.inn410.com

THE INN AT 410

Baked Pears

½ cup packed brown sugar
½ teaspoon cinnamon
¼ teaspoon mace
⅛ teaspoon ground cloves
4 large pears (preferably Anjou)
4 tablespoons butter or
    margarine
½ cup sour cream

½ tablespoon finely chopped
    crystallized ginger
¾ cup orange juice
Nutmeg to sprinkle

THE NIGHT BEFORE: The 'night before' directions can be done just before baking if you prefer, although the gingered sour cream should be mixed together ahead of time to allow the ginger flavor to permeate the sour cream.

Spray 9 inch × 13 inch baking pan with non-stick cooking spray. Spread brown sugar evenly on the bottom of the pan. Sprinkle with cinnamon, mace and cloves.

Peel pears, slice in half and remove core. Place pears cut side down on the sugar mixture. Dot with butter. Cover with foil and refrigerate overnight. Mix together sour cream and crystallized ginger. Refrigerate overnight in an airtight container. Mix up orange juice if necessary.

IN THE MORNING: Preheat oven to 350 degrees. Pour orange juice over the pears. Bake uncovered for 40 minutes or until pears are tender. Serve one pear half per person. Garnish with a dollop of the gingered sour cream and sprinkle with nutmeg.

Yield: 8 servings

CHALET SUZANNE INN

Broiled Grapefruit

1 grapefruit, at room
    temperature
3 tablespoon butter
1 teaspoon sugar

4 tablespoon cinnamon-sugar
    mixture (1 part cinnamon
    to 4 parts sugar)

Slice grapefruit in half and cut membrane around center of fruit. Cut around each section half, close to membrane, so that the fruit is completely loosened from its shell. Fill the center of each half with 1½ tablespoons butter. Sprinkle ½ teaspoon sugar over each half, then sprinkle each with 2 tablespoon cinnamon-sugar mixture. Place grapefruit on shallow baking pan and broil just long enough to brown tops and heat to bubbling hot. Remove from oven and serve hot.

Yield: 2 servings

CHALET SUZANNE
INN

3800 Chalet Suzanne Dr
Lake Wales, FL 33859

863-676-6011

EMAIL
info@chaletsuzanne.
com

URL
www.chaletsuzanne.
com

ASA RANSOM HOUSE

10529 Main St, Rt 5
Clarence, NY 14031

716-759-2315

EMAIL
innfo@asaransom.com

URL
www.asaransom.com

A S A   R A N S O M   H O U S E
Chocolate Peanut Butter Pie

Pastry:
1 cup chocolate wafer crumbs
½ cup chopped pecans
6 tablespoons unsalted, melted
    butter
2 tablespoons sugar
¼ teaspoon cinnamon
(or your favorite pre-baked pie
    crust)

Filling:
1¼ cups creamy peanut butter
1 8-ounce package softened
    cream cheese
1 cup powdered sugar
1 tablespoon vanilla
1¼ cups whipping cream

Glaze:
½ cup half & half or cream
4 ounces chopped semi-sweet
    chocolate

Can be made one day ahead. Mix all ingredients for pastry and press firmly in 10 inch pie pan. Freeze while preparing filling.

Use electric mixer to beat peanut butter, cream cheese, ½ cup sugar in a large bowl. Using clean dry beaters, beat whipping cream with ½ cup sugar and vanilla till soft peaks form. Stir ½ of cream mixture into peanut butter mixture. Fold well, then fold in the remaining cream mixture. Filling will be thick, so spread carefully into prepared crust and refrigerate till firm.

Bring cream to a boil, reduce heat and stir in chocolate till smooth and melted. Cool slightly and pour over filling, tilting pie pan for even distribution. Coat top of pie completely and refrigerate for 1 hour. Garnish with whipped cream and chocolate curls and enjoy!

Yield: 8 servings

ANNIVERSARY INN
Blueberry Peach Cobbler

4 cups sliced fresh or frozen
    peaches
¾ cup sugar
2 cups fresh or frozen
    blueberries
½ teaspoon almond extract

Topping:
¾ cup quick oats
¼ cup brown sugar
⅓ cup flour
4 tablespoons melted butter
⅛ teaspoon salt
¼ teaspoon cinnamon
¼ teaspoon nutmeg

ANNIVERSARY INN

1060 Mary's Lake Rd
Estes Park, CO 80517

970-586-6200

EMAIL
steers12@msn.com

URL
www.EstesInn.com

Combine peaches, sugar, blueberries and almond extract in a large bowl. Place equally in 3 inch individual ramekins or one large baking dish. Combine topping oats, brown sugar, flour, salt, cinnamon and nutmeg in a small bowl. Spread topping over fruit. Pour melted butter over topping. Place ramekins or baking dish on a greased baking pan and bake at 350 degrees for 30 minutes. Juices may spill over sides. Place ramekins on individual plates or dish out portions and serve.

Fruit and topping may be made a day ahead. Ramekins or baking dish should be covered and refrigerated. Dry topping should be sealed and stored at room temperature. The next morning add the topping, pour on the melted butter and bake.

Yield: 8 servings

OAK SQUARE B&B

1207 Church St
Port Gibson, MS 39150

601-437-5300

EMAIL
oaksquarebandb@
cs.com

O A K   S Q U A R E   B & B

Lazy Acre Praline

1 pkg vanilla pudding (kind you cook)
1½ cups firmly packed brown sugar
1 Tbsp butter
½ cup evaporated milk
2 cups pecan halves

Combine pudding, brown sugar, butter and milk in heavy pan. Heat slowly and stir constantly until sugar dissolves. Continue cooking to 238 degrees or until mixture forms a soft ball in cold water. Stir in pecans and beat for 2 or 3 minutes or until thickens. Drop onto wax paper. If it thickens too fast while dropping onto paper, heat over hot water.

This is a very easy and delicious recipe.

THE INN AT STARLIGHT LAKE

Award Winning Sour Cream Apple Pie

THE INN AT
STARLIGHT LAKE

PO Box 27
Starlight, PA 18461

570-798-2519

EMAIL
info@innatstarlightlake.
com

URL
www.innatstarlightlake.
com

Topping:
⅔ cup brown sugar
⅔ cup flour
2 tsp. cinnamon
¼ cup soft butter

Filling:
4 Tbsp. flour
¼ tsp salt
1⅓ cups sugar
2 eggs (med)
2 cups sour cream
1 tsp vanilla extract
½ tsp nutmeg
6 medium apples, peeled and shredded

Preheat oven to 400 degrees. Combine filling and place in a deep dish 10 inch pie shell. Place pie in oven for 10 minutes. Reduce heat to 350 degrees continue baking for 45 minutes or until pie is set. Add crumb topping and bake an additional 10 minutes at 400 degrees.

Yield: 10 servings

Cooking Time: 1 hr 5 min

THE LILAC INN

53 Park St
Brandon, VT 05733

802-247-5463

EMAIL
innkeeper@lilacinn.com

URL
www.lilacinn.com

THE LILAC INN
Lilac Inn Strawberry Rhubarb Pie

Crust for 2 crust pie   *3 cups diced rhubarb*
3 cups strawberries   *2 Tbsp. flour*
1½ cups sugar   *1 Tbsp. butter*
2 pie crusts   *Powdered sugar*
3 Tbsp. cornstarch

Cap and clean berries, slice into halves and place into medium size sauce pan. Add ½ cup sugar, mashing slightly to extract juice.

Stir cornstarch into a little cold water until smooth. Add to the berries. Cook gently until clear and juice is thickened.

Spread rhubarb over 1 pie crust in baking dish. Sprinkle with flour and 1 cup sugar. Dot with butter.

When berry mixture is slightly cooled, pour over rhubarb. Cover with pie crust and press edges together to seal

Slit top in a few places. Bake in 450 oven for 10 mins

Reduce to 350 for 30 mins

Yield: 6 servings

THE FIRELIGHT INN ON
OREGON CREEK

Firelight Blueberry Buckle

THE FIRELIGHT INN
ON OREGON CREEK

2211 E Third St
Duluth, MN 55812

218-724-0272

EMAIL
info@firelightinn.com

URL
www.firelightinn.com

¼ cup (½ stick) butter, softened
¾ cup granulated sugar
1 egg
1½ cups all-purpose flour
2 tsp baking powder
½ tsp salt
¼ tsp ground nutmeg
½ cup milk
2 cups fresh blueberries

Topping:
½ cup granulated sugar
⅓ cup all-purpose flour
¼ cup butter (½ stick)
½ tsp cinnamon

Preheat oven to 375 degrees. Cream butter and sugar. Blend in egg. In another bowl, mix flour, baking powder, salt and nutmeg. Add the flour mixture alternately with milk to creamed mixture. Gently fold in blueberries. Pour into greased 8 inch square pan. For topping combine ingredients and cut in butter. Sprinkle over batter. Bake 40–45 minutes. Cool on a rack.

Yield: 6 servings

CAMELLIA INN

211 North St
Healdsburg, CA 95448

707-433-8182

EMAIL
info@camelliainn.com

URL
www.camelliainn.com

C A M E L L I A I N N

Rhubarb Torte

1½ cups flour
4 tablespoons powder sugar
2¼ cups sugar
1 tablespoon vanilla
4 tablespoons flour
¾ cup butter (cut in pieces)
5 large stalks rhubarb (about 3 cups diced)
4 eggs
¼ teaspoon salt

Heat oven to 350 degrees.

Grease an 11 inch × 15 inch baking pan or casserole. In food processor, process flour, powdered sugar and butter until it starts to come together—approximately 1 minute. Press into bottom of pan and bake for 20 minutes.

Dice rhubarb. Process sugar, eggs, vanilla and salt until thick. Add flour and process 10 seconds. Stir into rhubarb and spread over crust.

Bake until top is brown and firm—35 minutes.

Cool completely before serving.

Cut into squares.

Yield: 2 dozen

CABERNET INN

Fantasy Fondue

⅔ *cup half & half*
¼ *cup granulated sugar*
8 oz semisweet chocolate chips (about 1½ cups)
1 Tbsp butter or margarine
½ tsp rum extract

Stir half & half and sugar in a medium saucepan over low heat until sugar dissolves. Add chocolate, stir over low heat until chocolate is melted and mixture is smooth. Remove from heat. Stir in butter until melted. Stir in extract.

Makes 2 cups.

To serve: prepare chocolate fondue and pour into fondue pot, keeping the pot warm with sterno. Cut up fruit and pound cake into bite-size pieces. Arrange on a glass plate next to the fondue pot. Provide guests with dessert plates and fondue forks, allowing them to select fruit and cake to dip into the fondue using the forks provided.

*Will keep up to one month in a tightly covered glass jar. To reheat, remove lid and place jar in a saucepan of simmering water. Stir occasionally until warm.

CABERNET INN

PO Box 489
North Conway, NH
03860

603-356-4704

EMAIL
info@cabernetinn.com

URL
www.cabernetinn.com

PAMELA LANIER

Aunt Carrie's Hungarian Coffee Cake

1 cup white sugar
1 cup brown sugar
1 cup butter or margarine
3 cups all-purpose flour
½ cup chopped nuts (optional)
1½ teaspoons cinnamon
1 cup buttermilk

2 eggs
1 teaspoon vanilla
½ teaspoon salt
1 teaspoon baking powder
1 teaspoon baking soda

Preheat oven to 350°F. Combine first six ingredients. Take out 1 level cup and set aside for topping. To the rest of the mixture add the remaining ingredients. Mix will be slightly lumpy.

    Pour into 8" cake or pie pans (2 or 3). Cover with the reserved nut mix and bake at 350°F for 20 or 25 minutes. Do not overbake. Will stay fresh for 4 days.

Yield: 6–8 servings

*I'm too busy visiting inns to own one, but like a lot of people, I've dreamed of becoming an innkeeper. If you share the dream of opening your own inn we have a great deal of practical information for prospective innkeepers written by many experts in the field on our website. Please visit us at **www.lanierbb.com** and click on "innkeeper resources." The website is filled with information about our member inns their special offers for our readers and, best of all, we add new recipes from innkeeper's everyday. Enjoy!*

– Pamela Lanier